THE LAUGHTER PRESCRIPTION

THE LAUGHTER PRESCRIPTION

The Tools of Humor and How to Use Them

DR. LAURENCE J. PETER
& BILL DANA

ILLUSTRATED BY NORMAN KLEIN

A publication of
The Light Stuff Company,
in association with
Dana/Corwin

BALLANTINE BOOKS · NEW YORK

All rights reserved under International and Pan-American Copyright Conventions. Published in the United States by Ballantine Books, a division of Random House, Inc., New York, and simultaneously in Canada by Random House of Canada Limited, Toronto, Canada

Library of Congress Cataloging in Publication Data

Peter, Laurence J.
    The laughter prescription.

    "A Dana/Corwin publication."
    Bibliography: p.
    1. Wit and humor—Therapeutic use.   2. Laughter—
Therapeutic use.   3. Success.   4. Mental health.
5. Health   I. Dana, Bill.   II. Title.
BF575.L3P47   1982   158   82-11379
ISBN 0-345-35333-1

The authors are grateful to the following for permission to quote or adapt from previously published material:

DELACORTE PRESS/SEYMOUR LAWRENCE: an excerpt from *Palm Sunday* by Kurt Vonnegut, Copyright © 1981 by The Ramjac Corporation.

Norman Cousins: material derived from *Anatomy of an Illness*, W.W. Norton & Co., Inc. 1979.

HEADWATERS PRESS: material adapted from *Laugh After Laugh: The Healing Power of Humor* by Dr. Raymond A. Moody, 1978.

Herbert Benson, M.D.: material derived from *The Relaxation Response*, William Morrow & Co., Inc., 1976.

Thanks, also, to John Yeck of The Let's Have Better Mottoes Association, Inc.; P.O. Box 225; Dayton Ohio 45401.

Manufactured in the United States of America

Designed by Helene Berinsky

First Edition: November 1982
10 9 8

Acknowledgments

●●

We gratefully acknowledge the enormous contributions of Editor Meg Staahl and Art Director Norman Klein of The Light Stuff Company; and thank Marc Jaffe, Dick Krinsley and Katie Sheehan of Ballantine for their faith in the future of therapeutic laughter.

L.P., B.D.

*From Laurence and Bill with love
to our wives, Irene and Evelyn,
necessarily in that order.*

Contents

●●●

Introduction

●●●

by Steve Allen

The human predicament being as notoriously difficult as it is, the preciousness of laughter is readily perceived. Arguments can arise as to which professional humorists or comedians are, or are not, particularly adept, but surely there would be little debate that both Laurence J. Peter and Bill Dana have done more than their share of providing laughter to a troubled world. If Dr. Peter had done nothing more than introduce his famous principle, even as an abstract philosophical statement, his perpetual fame would have been assured. But he has, in repeated instances, enlarged upon his central theme to hilarious effect. One of the particularly endearing things about his humor is that it is related to reality. He utilizes the actual components of life on planet earth and makes us see the humorous factor in all of it.

As for Bill Dana, I have selfish reasons to be pleased at the extent of his gifts, since he served as a member of my television writing staff for several years. He might still be toiling in such relative obscurity, in fact, were it not that I was finally able to induce him to perform some of his own routines publicly, one happy result of which was that his original characterization, José Jimenez, became a national favorite almost over night.

So popular were Bill and his alter-ego that shortly thereafter, in fact, the Danny Thomas production company prepared a situation comedy series for him.

I don't know how my two friends were brought together and perhaps it does not matter.

The reader will shortly note that what follows is by no means just another joke book, of the sort that is published every year. In the case of the present work, Messrs. Peter and Dana are up to something more important. Like Norman Cousins, they have perceived the therapeutic value of laughter. I suppose we would all agree that even if laughter were nothing more than sheer silliness and fun, it would still be a precious boon. But we now know that it is far more than that, that it is—in fact—an essential element in emotional health.

It is also a remarkably useful thing in the context of the whole process of human communication in that it is an aid to the expression of other emotions and to the transmission of important messages of spiritual, political, educational or commercial nature. It is, come to think of it, an absolute necessity in the maintenance of sanity. The authors, therefore, place the many examples of humor that they have chosen in the context of that general philosophical truth. The result is that the individual words, phrases, pictures and jokes that induce laughter are appreciated on at least two levels.

Although Bill Dana is one of the nation's top jokesmiths, he has, in this instance, wisely culled a good part of the cream-of-the-crop from various sources stretching back almost to the beginning of the century. One will find here echoes of Smith and Dale, Henny Youngman, the top comedy shows of radio's heyday, the 1930s, good lines from early TV sketches, even a few from my old shows. The working plan is clear. Dr. Peter sets up the essential philosophical principle and Mr. Dana supplies the bulk of the supporting documentation. The result is a refreshing formulation that can be literally guaranteed to induce anything from a wry smile to a loud guffaw on every page.

Unless he is an absolute glutton for the delicious flavor of laughter, the reader will probably not consume this book at one sitting. But it's a marvelous bedside companion, and a law should probably be passed requiring that it be given to every hospital patient in the English-speaking world.

The book is, moreover, a sort of how-to manual, since it includes a chapter on the development of one's sense of humor, the technique of writing jokes, the art of performing them and—even more importantly—the creation of a lifestyle in which humor is a conscious and significant element.

PART I

Health, Wealth and Happiness

●●

**The Picture of Health
Requires a
Happy Frame of Mind**

I.

The Best Medicine

●●

*The best doctors in the world
are Dr. Diet, Dr. Quiet and
Dr. Merryman*
— JONATHAN SWIFT

Early in my teaching career a student said to me, "Dr. Peter, you
must be greater than Einstein. I don't understand Einstein very
well, but I don't understand you at all." I appreciated the humor
of his remark and got the message. Experience taught me that
laughter in the classroom created a positive emotional climate, it
also made both teaching and learning easier and more effective.
Later, as a psychologist, I encountered clients who were able to
use humor as a way of coping with their problems and illnesses.
This led to my use of humor as a therapeutic method. Later still,
as an author, it seemed natural to use humor as my way of
communicating.

Laughter is the shortest distance between two people.
— VICTOR BORGE

When I wanted to write about a serious problem—the generally
held belief that the higher up the ladder, the better off we are—
I wrote a satirical book, *The Peter Principle*, in collaboration
with Raymond Hull.* The book was based on my observation of

---

*A description of each book referred to in text will be found in a
self-help section following parts I, II, III and IV.

corporate life—that in a hierarchy, individuals tend to rise to their levels of incompetence. I successfully communicated my message so that now, whenever I wish to convey a serious message, I frequently write it as satire, or as "Laws."

> *Peter's Financial Law:* Starting from scratch is easy; it's starting without it that's tough.
> *Peter's Educational Law:* Experience is the worst teacher; it gives the test before explaining the lesson.
> *Peter's Leadership Law:* Success comes to he who can blow his own horns while blowing others' minds.

As I continued to develop my own use of humor in teaching, in therapy and in communication, I began exploring how others were applying the panacea of laughter. I became convinced that, although one of the most ancient and widespread health beliefs of mankind was the therapeutic value of laughter, understanding how to use it was not common knowledge.

In this age of high-technology, scientific miracles and medical breakthroughs, it just might be that something as simple as laughter is the best medicine, after all. For a long time, medical doctors have known that happy patients generally respond more favorably to treatment and recover faster than do cheerless and complaining ones. The evidence suggests that laughter, confidence and hope have significant therapeutic value, while sadness, fear and despondency tend to produce negative outcomes.

The art of medicine consists of amusing the patient while nature cures the disease.
—VOLTAIRE

Often the cures attributed to humor are grouped along with mystical treatments and healing miracles. Our history is replete with stories of individuals healed by persons possessing "the magic touch," or other powers, who create healing miracles. People have gathered at special places where healing forces were reputed to be concentrated. These included religious shrines and locations where the waters were supposed to have healing properties, such as Lourdes in France, the Ganges in India, the Nile in Egypt and the Tigris in Iraq. Although recent investigations cast reasonable doubt about the authenticity of most of the cures, a few genuine cures have been discovered. Many individuals have said that they have been cured of fatal illnesses through prayer and divine intervention, and others have claimed that they have healed themselves through autosuggestion or the power of positive thinking. Whether or not these methods are effective is difficult to discern, because the number of persons using the techniques is unknown and the tendency is for only the alleged successes to be reported. The fact remains that people sometimes do recover from "incurable" diseases, and when such miracles happen the medical profession labels the recovery spontaneous remission.

> *I learned why they're called wonder drugs—you wonder what they'll do to you.*
> —HARLAN MILLER

We should not underestimate the value of faith healing and mind-over-matter cures. They can be important components of a comprehensive health plan, but by their very nature they are resistant to scientific analysis.

Humor, too, is difficult to analyze in the laboratory, and so research to date has been limited. Examination of available findings, however, indicates that the physical benefits of humor have a firm scientific basis. Dr. William F. Fry, Jr., M.D., an associate clinical professor at Stanford University Medical School, who has been studying the effects of humor on health for twenty-five years, says that if it were not for laughs we might be much sicker than we are. "Without our realizing it, day to day humor may be making a significant contribution to our physical well-being."

One of the most celebrated cases of laughter helping to combat serious illness is that of Norman Cousins, author and former long-time editor of the *Saturday Review* magazine. In his bestselling book *Anatomy of an Illness, As Perceived by the Patient: Reflections on Healing and Regeneration*, Cousins details his remarkable recovery from a potentially fatal illness. Following a stress-filled trip abroad, he suffered from a serious collagen disease, a disorder of the connective tissue. He experienced great pain and had difficulty moving. The prognosis for recovery was poor. With the understanding and cooperation of his doctor, he took charge of certain aspects of his own treatment, part of which consisted of humor therapy.

The witch doctor succeeds for the same reason all the
rest of us succeed. Each patient carries his own doctor
inside him. They come to us not knowing that truth.
We are best when we give the doctor who resides
within each patient a chance to go to work.
                                        —ALBERT SCHWEITZER

Cousins checked himself out of the hospital and into a more cheerful hotel room. He watched comedy films. He noted that one ten-minute interlude of laughter produced two hours of painless sleep. It was also discovered that each session of laughter caused a reduction in inflammation and that the effect was cumulative. His self-administered program also included a nutritious diet. His well-being was restored, and for more than fifteen years Norman Cousins has enjoyed vigorous good health.

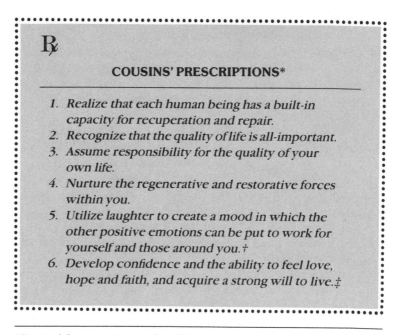

℞

COUSINS' PRESCRIPTIONS*

1. *Realize that each human being has a built-in capacity for recuperation and repair.*
2. *Recognize that the quality of life is all-important.*
3. *Assume responsibility for the quality of your own life.*
4. *Nurture the regenerative and restorative forces within you.*
5. *Utilize laughter to create a mood in which the other positive emotions can be put to work for yourself and those around you.†*
6. *Develop confidence and the ability to feel love, hope and faith, and acquire a strong will to live.‡*

*Derived from *Anatomy of an Illness*
†Cousins's specific ingredients were viewing Marx Brothers films and "Candid Camera" replays and reading humor books.
‡Ana Aslan, one of Rumania's leading endocrinologists, says there is a direct connection between a robust will to live and the chemical balances in the brain.

> *The mind is its own place and in itself can make a*
> *heaven of Hell, a hell of Heaven.*
>
> —JOHN MILTON

Two consequences of a sense of humor contribute to the restoration of physical health. The first is the ability to laugh at yourself, and the other is the act of laughter itself. Humor is the miracle drug with no bad side effects.

> *One of the new miracle drugs is inexpensive. That's the*
> *miracle.*
>
> —HAROLD COFFIN

Laughter produces beneficial physiological results. It exercises the lungs and stimulates the circulatory system. Hearty laughter causes full action of the diaphragm, the main muscle of respiration, situated between the chest and abdomen. The whole cardiovascular system benefits from robust laughter because the deep respiration that accompanies it increases the oxygen in the blood. This is of particular benefit to persons who have been inactive due to long-term or seriously debilitating illnesses.

Norman Cousins calls laughter a form of internal jogging. In responding to the initial phase of a typical joke, comedy routine or story, muscle tension increases in anticipation of the climax of the story or punchline. Immediately following the story climax, the thorax (chest), abdomen and face get a vigorous workout. In convulsive laughter, where the individual really breaks up, even the legs and arms are involved. During this phase, heart rate, breathing and circulation are speeded up. When the spasm of laughter subsides, the pulse rate drops below normal and the skeletal muscles become deeply relaxed. During the laughter response, the body is revitalized by what sometimes is called internal massage.

PAIN

Can we laugh our pains away? Maybe not, but we can use humor to gain control over pain. An athlete who receives an injury in the height of competition may not be aware of it until sometime later. Two arthritis patients with the same degree of physical degeneration may experience vastly different degrees of pain. A person's perception of pain is influenced by his/her belief system, expectations and self-image and a variety of unconscious psychological strategies.

> *Pain is an energy monster; we give it the power to hurt us. And we can take that power away—depending on how we choose to view ourselves. All pain is real, but you can change your reality.*
>
> —DAVID BLACK

Humor and laughter control pain in four major ways: (1) by distracting attention, (2) by reducing tension, (3) by changing expectations and (4) by increasing production of endorphins—the body's natural painkillers.

Attention

Aches and pains can intensify if attention is given to them. A degree of anesthesia can be achieved simply by drawing attention from the pain. At least for the moment, the laughing person pays little attention to the source of discomfort. Recently I had an attack of gout, an intensely painful condition affecting my left foot. As an experiment, I first attended to the pain. Then I watched *Sons of the Desert*, a Laurel and Hardy movie. After viewing the film, I again concentrated on my foot. The pain was greatly reduced and even the focusing of my attention on it did not cause it to return to its earlier intensity.

> *If you think you have caught a cold, call in a doctor...*
> *Call in three doctors and play bridge.*
>
> —ROBERT BENCHLEY

Relaxation

Laughter reduces muscle tension. An injury or disease may lead to unconscious tensing of the muscles around the affected part of the body, causing increased pain. Laughter causes muscle relaxation and is effective when tension exists. There are also painful conditions that result from muscle tension alone. Anxiety can cause tension in the neck and head muscles and produce a headache. When a person with one of these unconsciously self-generated headaches, backaches or other tension pain is made to laugh, the tension may be relieved.

> *I think the next best thing to solving a problem is finding some humor in it.*
>
> —FRANK A. CLARK

Dr. David Bresler, director of the University of California at Los Angeles's (UCLA's) Pain Control Unit, says that pain is the most common, expensive and disabling disorder in the United States and that to eliminate pain all you have to do is change your mind: "Almost always, people who have chronic pain are also depressed. It's not just their lower back that hurts; their life hurts, and they have placed that hurt in their lower back."

Attitude
An individual's general outlook or attitude toward life is related to pain sensitivity. Positive expectations and the will to recover from illness are not very well understood, but many medical practitioners report that they appear to be related to pain tolerance. At least we can be quite sure that laughter and a sense of humor are related to a positive attitude and the will to live.

> *I am more important than my problems.*
> —JOSÉ FERRER

Endorphins
Recent and encouraging evidence suggests that humor may directly attack the pain associated with inflammatory conditions such as arthritis, gout and those resulting from certain injuries. Mirth and laughter stimulate the brain to produce catecholamine—the alertness hormone, a complex substance that includes epinephrine, norepinephrine and dopamine which prepare us to respond physically for either fight or flight. The arousal hormone in turn stimulates release of endorphins—our natural painkillers. As the level of endorphins in the brain increases, the perception of pain decreases. Laughter, then, causes our bodies to produce our own painkillers. It has also been evidenced that the increased level of catecholamines in the blood can reduce inflammation.

> *The sound body is the product of the sound mind.*
> —GEORGE BERNARD SHAW

We have seen that laughter can stimulate the cardiovascular system, that it can produce deep muscle relaxation, which promotes healing, and that it can help control pain. But a sense of humor is more than just laughter. Psychologically, the ability to see the humor in a situation is as important as the laughter itself.

An individual with a good sense of humor is one who can take a comic view of life's trials and tribulations. One must be able to step back from a situation and view it with a degree of detachment. Separating yourself from an annoying incident is the constructive way of breaking the vicious cycle that causes depression: As we experience annoyances or disappointments, our mirthfulness decreases. This may cause us biochemically to become depressed, and may, in turn, further dampen our sense of humor, so that we laugh less and continue the downward spiraling pattern of depression.

A healthy sense of humor can rescue us from life's inevitable setbacks. If we can say "This situation is absurd," we may arrest the depression process and escape the immobilization caused by further depression.

A Surgeon's Book of Hope, by Dr. William A. Nolen, describes patients upon whom surgery was performed and who made remarkable recoveries, even when the prognosis was poor. Nolen concludes that much of what determines the outcome of an illness is beyond the understanding and control of the physician. Implicit in this acknowledgment is the reality that we and our doctors are unable to predict precisely the outcome of any illness or the results of any treatment. In comparison with something as precise as surgery, humor therapy is quite vague and the results are even more unpredictable.

> *Our doctor would never really operate unless it was*
> *necessary. He was just that way. If he didn't need the*
> *money, he wouldn't lay a hand on you.*
>
> **—HERB SHRINER**

In his book *Laugh after Laugh: The Healing Power of Humor*, Dr. Raymond Moody discusses the clinical evidence supporting the therapeutic benefits of laughter, but he also points out the lack of solid research into humor therapy. Although the evidence he presents in favor of humor is mainly of the case-study type, he does make certain recommendations. When a doctor dispenses laughter to a patient, he increases the quality of the patient's life. Dr. Moody does not propose that doctors become comedians but that they abandon some of their professional solemnity and help their patients take a more humorous perspective. He does not recommend that doctors replace traditional medical techniques with humor but that the techniques be supplemented with humor therapy.

In terms of our present knowledge, Dr. Moody's book presents a professionally responsible position. With all of the clinical evidence of the benefits of laughter in facilitating the healing process, it would be irresponsible not to recommend its use. On the other hand, lacking definitive knowledge and research about the specific kinds of humor and for which conditions they may be beneficial, the responsible position is to regard humor as an adjunct to the more specific forms of therapy, such as diet, medication and surgery.

℞

PETER'S HUMOR THERAPY PRESCRIPTION.

1. *Follow your doctor's advice.*
2. *Acquire positive expectations of health.*
3. *Laugh it up.*

In the humor sections following each chapter, you will find a sample of jokes, articles and cartoons which, as Bill observes, he has "written, remembered and arranged." I have prescribed humor as a useful treatment of our illnesses and woes. The estimable Mr. Dana is the pharmacist who fills this prescription.

GENIAL HOSPITAL

A hospital is a rotten place to be sick. It's also a tough work environment. Some patients have registered complaints about the black "M*A*S*H" humor they've observed nearby their ailing bodies. They shouldn't. What they evaluate as medicarelessness actually helps the survival of those professionals who must cope with hospital stress. This gives the patient a healthier doctor, nurse or whoever to look after his/her needs. Or it doesn't. In which case, turn the clowns in to the commanding officer.

"I'm a little worried about your husband. I don't like the way he looks."
"Neither do I, but he's good to the kids."

After two days in the hospital, I took a turn for the nurse.

—W.C. FIELDS

Houston—(The L.P. Times)—The medical community was thrilled today to learn that researchers have discovered a cure for which there is no known disease.

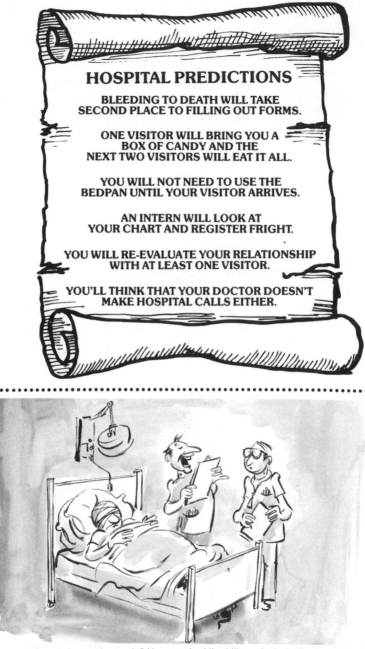

HOSPITAL PREDICTIONS

BLEEDING TO DEATH WILL TAKE
SECOND PLACE TO FILLING OUT FORMS.

ONE VISITOR WILL BRING YOU A
BOX OF CANDY AND THE
NEXT TWO VISITORS WILL EAT IT ALL.

YOU WILL NOT NEED TO USE THE
BEDPAN UNTIL YOUR VISITOR ARRIVES.

AN INTERN WILL LOOK AT
YOUR CHART AND REGISTER FRIGHT.

YOU WILL RE-EVALUATE YOUR RELATIONSHIP
WITH AT LEAST ONE VISITOR.

YOU'LL THINK THAT YOUR DOCTOR DOESN'T
MAKE HOSPITAL CALLS EITHER.

"Cranial puncture, eh? He needed that like a hole in the head."

FUNNY BONES

"Hi, you're new on this staff, aren't you?"

Ever wonder why doctors are almost consistently referred to as "doctor" but no other profession is thusly dignified? Why not Lr. Smith, the lawyer; Br. Jones, the banker; or Pr. Johnson, the plumber? Perhaps we need the security created by the sense of authority and parental concern engendered by the use of the title Doctor. Actually, anyone whom we respect should be addressed by an appropriate title. I was telling that just the other day to Ronnie Reagan.

—AMOS ANON

MY FRIEND WAS OPERATED ON FOR KIDNEY TROUBLE AND FOUR DAYS LATER HE DIED OF HEART TROUBLE.

MY DOCTOR IS A SPECIALIST, IF HE OPERATES FOR KIDNEY TROUBLE, YOU DIE OF KIDNEY TROUBLE AND IT DON'T TAKE NO FOUR DAYS EITHER!

"Are all these people ahead of me?"
"Yes, but you can go right in."
"That's all right. I've got lots of time."
"No you don't—I've seen your X-rays."

"Your wife has extreme hypertensions and all the consulting doctors recommend the same thing—that your wife have sex at least fives times a month."

"Terrific—put me down for two."

Today *The Laughter Prescription* is proud to salute Dr. F. Feeney Fernlaw, for his remarkable discovery of the drug Fernamiacin, which cures the rare tropical disease known as Croccotosis. We are now pulling for you, Dr. Fernlaw, to come up with the side effect of the drug known as Fernlaw's Disease.

●

"How could that ¢*$#@* doctor charge so much?"

—HIPPOCRATIC OATH

"I'm slowly going crazy over the ladies."
"There's nothing wrong with that."

"I know...but could you speed it up?"

"You have nothing to worry about. You'll live to be sixty."
"I am sixty."
"What did I tell you?"

IV'E GOT THE GREATEST DOCTOR, IF HE CAN'T CURE YOU... HE'LL TOUCH UP THE X-RAYS!

"She got her good looks from her father. He's a plastic surgeon."

Doctor-Patient Relationship

DOCTOR, WHEN I GET OUT OF HERE I WANT TO MARRY A 20 YEAR OLD GIRL.

THAT COULD BE FATAL.

IF SHE DIES, SHE DIES.

"This medical report should put your wife's mind at ease. Let me read it to you. 'Dear Mrs. Levine, This is to certify that Mr. Levine can engage in sexual activities as often as he wishes. He is in remarkable condition. He has the strength and body of a twenty year old.'
"That's very good, except for one thing. Would you cross out Mrs. Levine and write 'To Whom It May Concern'?"

2.

Keeping Fit

●●●

If anything is sacred,
the human body is sacred.
——WALT WHITMAN

Staying healthy should be the easiest thing in the world. Your
body has great wisdom and is wonderfully equipped to take care
of itself. If you overexert yourself, your body lets you know it is
tired, and all you have to do is obey its message. Have a rest and
it will restore itself completely. You don't have to figure out
which cells need to be replaced or which toxic waste products
have to be removed. Just relax, and your wonderfully competent
body will do all the complex restoration work that's needed.

If you get a cut or a bruise, you don't have to think about how
you are going to heal the injury. The best qualified doctor in the
world wouldn't know exactly what your body needs to repair
the wound. Yet, your body goes to work and sends blood containing many different kinds of cells—each a unit of life with a
specific job to do—to the reconstruction site. The cells go to
work—some bring nutrients to sustain other cells; some break
down bacteria and carry it away; some produce antibodies; some
remove waste produced by other cells. The miracle of healing
takes place and you don't have to do anything about it.

Your body is so well and intricately designed that there is little
you can do to improve on its healing processes. You can, however,
interfere. You can fail to heed your body's messages and carry on

so that your wound receives further injury, or you can worry and become tense, which may impair blood flow to the injury. An unfortunate side effect of modern medicine is that we have lost faith in our own bodies' power to heal. If our back aches we go to a doctor, who prescribes bed rest. A primitive man would heed his body's messages and know what it needed.

Most of our preventable health problems are caused by not letting our bodies do what they want to do. They want a natural rhythm of exertion and relaxation, but we force them to work when tired. Despite the signals, we press on and then wonder why we become run-down. Our bodies want to function without undue stress, but we worry and fuss and become irritable, depressed and hypertense. We don't give ourselves a fair chance to achieve our wishes for a life filled with zest, vitality and happiness.

> *The best cure for hypochondria is to forget about your*
> *own body and get interested in someone else's.*
> —GOODMAN ACE

Medical researchers have focused on, and have been highly successful in developing, specific treatments for specific diseases and problems. Medications that destroy bacteria, surgery that repairs damaged organs and prosthetic devices that restore amputees to almost-normal functioning are but a few of the miracles of modern medicine.

> *Medicine, the only profession that labours incessantly*
> *to destroy the reason for its existence.*
> —JAMES BRYCE

In this chapter, we are not ignoring the importance of employing the best that modern medicine can offer, but are concentrating instead on a different goal—how to achieve positive wellness. To achieve optimum well-being you must look not just to your body in terms of symptoms of illness or of health but to your whole being, from physical, mental, emotional, spiritual and ecological points of view.

> *Let each become all that he was created capable of*
> *being; expand if possible, to his full growth; and show*
> *himself at length in his own shape and stature.*
> —THOMAS CARLYLE

BODY

Your body evolved, over a period of millions of years, through adaptations to a wide variety of environmental conditions. It survived because it was able to thrive on foods provided by the environment. The human species obtained food and shelter by exploring, foraging and hunting. These activities, along with sleep, provided all that was needed—food, exercise and rest.

In very recent times, we have made such rapid changes in our living conditions that our bodies have not had time to adapt. Your muscles and circulatory system are not ready for the life of inactivity provided by the automobile, television and labor-saving devices. Your digestive and metabolic systems are not capable of functioning effectively on a diet of refined foods devoid of complex nutrients and inundated with artificial colors, flavors, and preservatives.

> *The end of the human race will be that it will eventually die of civilization.*
>
> —**RALPH WALDO EMERSON**

The answer for the individual seems obvious. He/she must give up the popular diet that modern civilization has provided and return to eating unprocessed natural foods. This involves cutting back drastically on fats, and highly refined carbohydrates such as sugar and white flour.

> *The food here is so tasteless you could eat a meal of it and belch and it wouldn't remind you of anything.*
>
> —**REDD FOXX**

Your every cell, organ and body part grows in strength and function through regular exercise. The health of each cell—and therefore every part of your body—depends on the body's abundant supply of blood, rich in nutrients, distributed throughout your body by heart, muscles, arteries and capillaries. Daily vigorous exercise is an important ingredient in maintaining healthy blood flow.

> *Walking isn't a lost art—one must, by some means, get to the garage.*
>
> —**EVAN ESAR**

The recent popularity of the book *The Pritikin Program for Diet and Exercise*, by Nathan Pritikin with Patrick M. Grady, Jr., is an indication that there is a growing trend among people to become involved in their own health maintenance and illness prevention.

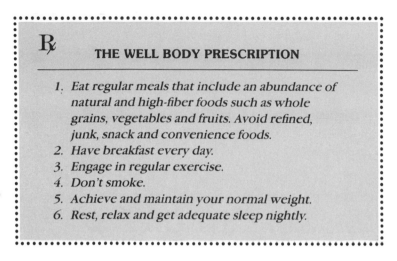

R̥   **THE WELL BODY PRESCRIPTION**

1. *Eat regular meals that include an abundance of natural and high-fiber foods such as whole grains, vegetables and fruits. Avoid refined, junk, snack and convenience foods.*
2. *Have breakfast every day.*
3. *Engage in regular exercise.*
4. *Don't smoke.*
5. *Achieve and maintain your normal weight.*
6. *Rest, relax and get adequate sleep nightly.*

MIND

The belief that the mind has good and bad effects on the body is as old as recorded history. Modern science supports the validity of the old belief that "As a man thinketh, so is he." It is also true that the body is developed and renewed by food, exercise and rest, not by thinking alone, no matter how noble that thinking is. Prolonged worry is destructive to all organs and interferes with the digestion and assimilation of even the best of food. Conversely, impaired bodily functions resulting from disease, overeating or overindulgence in alcohol will impair clear thinking. This mind-body, body-mind interaction constitutes a oneness; it is unrealistic to speak of something affecting only the body or only the mind.

> **What we steadily, consciously, habitually think we are, that we tend to become.**
> —JOHN COWPER POWERS

Although mental activity includes everything we are capable of thinking about, our concern here is thought and its relationship to health. One of the most obvious uses of the mind in this respect is in analyzing your life style and planning changes where habits are interfering with your health. The decision to cut down on drinking, quit smoking, lose weight or seek medical advice is an outcome of thinking about these problems. A second mental activity that contributes to health is thinking well of yourself. Healthful self-confidence includes a high level of self-esteem, along with the knowledge that your body is wonderfully made and is capable of warding off disease. This positive expectation of health is one mental activity that will pay dividends in both health and happiness.

A sense of humor is most helpful in maintaining positive expectations. Even the most physically and mentally healthy individual has disappointments that trigger the blues. When seen with a sense of humor, these traumas and stresses tend to pass quickly, and the individual soon will return to the peak of wellness. Mentally healthy individuals accept unexpected setbacks as a part of life. They don't waste time and effort worrying that their circumstances are not ideal. They simply make the best of their circumstances. They think about their problems. They make decisions. They act. Whatever the consequences, they know they did their best at the time.

Do what you can, with what you have, where you are.
—THEODORE ROOSEVELT

EMOTION

Proper nutrition, exercise, rest and mental attitude do a lot to reduce stress. If you are in good physical condition, you can handle the stresses of life effectively. Emotional stress can cause physical deterioration by setting off a complex process that starts in the cerebrum, the thinking part of the brain. Thoughts in the cerebrum can affect the hypothalamus, the part of the brain that regulates body temperature, certain metabolic processes, the autonomic nervous system and chemical balance. Your feelings literally can make you sick or well. Emotional stress is just as real as any kind of physical stress. When you experience sustained anxiety, anger or fear, your physical processes are out of balance and your body cells actually are deteriorating. If degenerative trends are not corrected, you will become susceptible to colds, coronaries and a host of diseases. It is, therefore, important that downward spirals be reversed immediately.

> *We crucify ourselves between two thieves; regret for yesterday and fear of tomorrow.*
>
> —FULTON OURSLER

There are two effective ways you can get immediate relief from emotional stress. One is laughter, and the other is deep relaxation. You can summon laughter by listening to a comedy recording, watching a movie or television comedy or attending a live comic performance. Comedy records, audio cassette tapes, videodiscs or cassettes and films can be made part of a home collection or can be borrowed from commercial or public libraries for private viewing or listening.

Record Albums

Nearly all of the great comedians make recordings of their performances, so you can hear your favorites whenever you wish. Some of my favorites are *Woody Allen* (Woody Allen, Colpix Records SCP 518); *Bette Midler Live at Last* (Bette Midler and the Harlettes, Atlantic SD2–9000); *The Two and Only* (Bob Elliott and Ray Goulding, Columbia S30412); *Here's Jonathan* (Jonathan Winters, Verve V15025); *Mark Twain Tonight* (Hal Holbrook, Columbia OS 2019); *Tony Randall* (Tony Randall, Imperial Records, Inc. LP 12034); *Improvisations to Music* (Mike Nichols and Elaine May, Mercury SR 60040); *On the Road* (George Carlin, Little David LD 1075); *An Evening with Tom Lehrer* (Tom Lehrer, Reprise 6199); *I Am Not a Nut* (Lenny Bruce, Fantasy 7007); *The World of British Comedy* (Marty Feldman, Spike Milligan, Benny Hill, Peter Cook, Dudley Moore and others, Decca PA 39); *Freakin' at the Freakers Ball* (Shel Silverstein, Columbia KC 31119); *An Evening with Groucho* (Groucho Marx, A&M Records SP 3515); *The Best of José* (available from Bill Dana Enterprises: 2029 Century Park East, Suite 1850, Los Angeles, CA. 90067).

These are but a few of the records that have stood the test of time for me. You will have to be judge of what you find enduringly amusing.

The recorded performance that you enjoy hearing again and again will become the core of your collection. Many of the vintage routines of the great comedians have achieved that status in my collection. Some of the best performances of comics such as Eddie Cantor, Fred Allen, Ed Wynn, George Burns and Gracie Allen, Fanny Brice, Allan Sherman, Red Skelton, Oscar Levant, Ernie Kovacs, Leonard Barr, Woody Woodbury, Bob Hope, Fibber McGee and Molly are contained in the five-record set *The Golden Age of Comedy* (The Longine Symphonette Society LS 210A).

W.C. Fields's famous "Temperance Lecture" and the songs of Mae West are included in *W.C. Fields and Mae West* (Proscenium 22).

Original radio broadcasts from the period of great radio comedy, including complete half-hour shows by Abbott and Costello, Jack Benny, Burns and Allen, The Great Gildersleeve, Eddie Cantor, Edgar Bergen, Jimmy Durante and Amos and Andy, are available in a five-record set, *The Great Radio Comedians* (Murray Hill Records 931699).

Movies

Those who have movie projection equipment or those to whom it is available can show a wide selection of comedy films through purchase, rental, lease or through the lending services of the public libraries.

Films from the past as well as recent films are being transferred to videotape cassettes and discs for showing on home video recorders or players.

A listing of sources of comedy films is beyond the scope of this chapter, but for the potential borrower many libraries have the reference book *Feature Films in 8MM, 16MM, and Videotape: A Directory of Feature Films Available for Rental, Sale and Lease in the U.S.A. and Canada*, by James L. Limbacker (R.R. Bowker & Co., 1180 Avenue of the Americas, New York, New York 10036).

For those who want to purchase their favorite films or videotapes, Blackhawk Films (Box 3990, 1235 West 5th Street, Davenport, Iowa 52808) provides an extensive catalogue on request.

My favorites are the films from the golden age of comedy and some of the more recent pictures made in the style of that era.

CHARLIE CHAPLIN

Many great comedians contributed to the art of motion-picture comedy, but none made quite the impact of Charlie Chaplin. He was the writer, director, producer, composer and distributor of many films in which he starred. His films show the development of comedy from slapstick to satire. Chaplin made comedies for years before he established the fully rounded character of the little tramp.

The Gold Rush, 1925. This comic masterpiece contains many classic scenes: Charlie on the verge of starvation, eating his boot, his cabin on the move, his fantasy about the beautiful girls and many more. Although it was filmed as a silent picture, versions are available with a Chaplin narration and musical score.

City Lights, 1931. This film, and those that followed, reveal a complex Chaplin who could use his comedy to make strong social commentary while being very funny.

Modern Times, 1936. This film brings together all the elements that made Chaplin the most universally popular entertainer in the world. He is the victim of automation and the boom and bust economy, but he survives a breakdown, false imprisonment and poverty and, in the end, walks toward the horizon hand in hand with his girl; hope is in their hearts.

BUSTER KEATON

The comedian making the most innovative use of film was Buster Keaton. He had been a clever on-stage performer and acrobat, but movies provided the medium for his creative talents. He created stunts that could only be accomplished by use of the camera. Trick shots and special setups made the impossible seem easy.

Cops, 1922. When Buster tries a business venture to impress his girlfriend, the result is one of the best-plotted and -executed chase scenes ever planned—a comedy classic.

The Blacksmith, 1922. Keaton burlesques Longfellow's famous poem, "The Village Blacksmith."

Other Keaton greats include *One Week*, 1920; *The General*, 1926; *College*, 1927; *Steamboat Bill*, 1928 and *The Silent Partner*, 1955.

THE MARX BROTHERS

When this team moved from vaudeville and the Broadway stage

to Hollywood, a new kind of movie was born. The brothers starred in a series of the zaniest comedies ever recorded on film.

Animal Crackers, 1930. This film version of their Broadway success established them as movie stars. It contains one of Groucho's great musical numbers, "Hooray for Captain Spaulding."

Monkey Business, 1931. In this ship-board romp, Zeppo's girlfriend is kidnapped and madness breaks out when Groucho, Harpo and Chico come to the rescue. Even Groucho's Depression-era puns still make me laugh.

Horse Feathers, 1932. Groucho, as president of a university, tries to lead his school to football victory over rival Huxley University. The gags fly faster than the ball.

Duck Soup, 1933. Groucho as Rufus T. Firefly, the mad monarch of the mythical kingdom of Freedonia, leads his country through crazy, hilarious, anarchic troubles. It can be viewed as political satire pointing out the insanity of war.

A Night at the Opera, 1935. The Marx version of *Il Trovatore* closes this madcap romp through dozens of hilarious moments, thus concluding their funniest film.

OTHERS

Some W.C. Fields films, Laurel and Hardy films, and many of the Little Rascals, Abbott and Costello, Charley Chase, Mae West and Harold Lloyd films are available. Modern classics of comedy, including the films of Woody Allen and Mel Brooks, can also be obtained for home viewing. There is something available to suit almost every taste.

Books, Articles and Cartoons

If comedy movies and records represent areas too vast to describe meaningfully, then a description of available humorous literature is virtually impossible. The humor section of your library or bookstore contains a variety of joke books, cartoon books, satires and humorous novels or short stories for you to choose from. Experience is your only reliable guide to what will raise your spirits and make you laugh. Some individuals, when under stress, can still respond with mirth and laughter to cartoons or humorous literature. Others respond more readily to humor in movies, television or live performances. Whatever your source for laughter, it will unleash your stress.

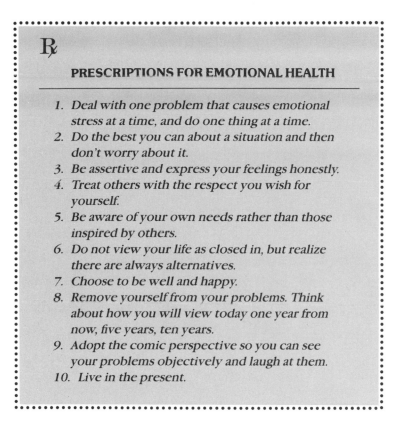

℞

PRESCRIPTIONS FOR EMOTIONAL HEALTH

1. *Deal with one problem that causes emotional stress at a time, and do one thing at a time.*
2. *Do the best you can about a situation and then don't worry about it.*
3. *Be assertive and express your feelings honestly.*
4. *Treat others with the respect you wish for yourself.*
5. *Be aware of your own needs rather than those inspired by others.*
6. *Do not view your life as closed in, but realize there are always alternatives.*
7. *Choose to be well and happy.*
8. *Remove yourself from your problems. Think about how you will view today one year from now, five years, ten years.*
9. *Adopt the comic perspective so you can see your problems objectively and laugh at them.*
10. *Live in the present.*

Laughter is the sensation of feeling good all over, and showing it principally in one place.

—JOSH BILLINGS

SPIRIT

Spirit is that which constitutes one's unseen, intangible being or one's essential activating principle. Spirit, as used here, implies that human life is more than the sum of physical parts—such as brain, muscles, skin and intestines—along with mind and emotion. Spirit refers to that which gives meaning and purpose to life. Spiritual growth is part of the actualization of human potential. It leads to deep inner satisfaction, happiness and enlightenment.

R⁄

PRESCRIPTION FOR EXPANDING CONSCIOUSNESS AND FOR BROADENING SPIRITUAL HORIZONS

1. *Spend time alone. Regularly have a time of silence by yourself, in which you engage in quiet contemplation, silent prayer or meditation. Courses in transcendental meditation (TM) are available in most major cities and are recommended for those who have not acquired other ways to find complete relaxation and tranquility.*
2. *Accept responsibility for your own happiness. You, and you alone, must determine your real needs and fulfill them.*
3. *Develop balance and harmony in your life. Your work, rest and recreation should form a balanced rest-activity cycle. Your physical, mental and emotional life should interact in harmonious support of one another.*
4. *Accept the reality of your own death. Recognition of your own mortality is a liberating experience that awakens you to your responsibility to savor every moment.*
5. *Develop a personal philosophy of life that sustains you on your quest for self-actualization or fulfillment. Do not strive for a perfect philosophy that has all the answers, but be satisfied with one that gives purpose to your life, even if it doesn't answer the big question of the purpose of all life.*
6. *Keep growing.*

ECOLOGY

When does the environment become *you?* When you breathe in, does the air become you? Is it you when it is inside your lungs? Or is it only you when absorbed into your blood cells? The air you exhale contains carbon dioxide and other products of your body. When does that air become something apart from you? When you exhale? When it leaves the cells? When it leaves the lungs? What about food and drink? When is it you and when is it environment?

These questions do not have ready answers. To other persons, animals and plants, you are part of their environment, so when we speak of man and his environment, man is also that environment.

> *Western man labors under the infinitely satisfying and destructive delusion that there is something special about him that makes him independent of his environment. What he must come to realize is that—contrary to all the teachings about his "divine right" and his unique place in the cosmos—he is just a parasite. Man is totally dependent on his environment.*
>
> **—IAN L. MacHARG**

Modern technology has produced a new set of environmental factors that are seriously threatening your health. Pesticides, plastics and certain food additives are among the substances that are suspected carcinogens. Fluorocarbons are destroying the protective ozone layer in the atmosphere. Air pollution is causing, or at least contributing to, emphysema and other lung diseases. We are exposed continually to noxious agents including acid rain, toxic chemicals and noise pollution.

> *The sun, the moon, and the stars would have disappeared long ago, had they happened to be within reach of predatory human hands.*
>
> **—HAVELOCK ELLIS**

The problems of how we can learn to live in harmony with our fellow humans and our natural environment are beyond the scope of this book. *Human Life Styling: Keeping Whole in the 20th Century*, by John C. McCamy, M.D., and James Presley, will be of interest to those who want a life style that improves health and that also protects the environment.

R̸

PERSONAL ENVIRONMENTAL PRESCRIPTION

1. Keep medicines and other chemical agents, such as cleaning products, plant food and pesticides, out of the reach of children.
2. Avoid chemical deodorants that clog pores and prevent the normal functions of the skin.
3. Avoid synthetic clothes, particularly undergarments, because synthetic fibers do not breathe as do natural fibers, and thus cause an imbalance of skin bacteria that results in skin disorders. Buy clothes made of at least 50 percent cotton or wool.
4. Avoid smoke-filled rooms, toxic fumes, smog and other environmental pollutants.
5. Take camping trips and go on hikes where the air is clean and fresh.
6. Eliminate safety hazards in and around the home.
7. Keep a list of the numbers of the fire department and police, hospital emergency, poison center, paramedics and family doctor near the telephone.

HOLISTIC HEALTH

The integration of the physical, mental, emotional, spiritual and ecological components of the human being constitutes a holistic approach to health. Holism is the name of an ancient theory that the universe, and particularly living things, are more than a sum of their parts. Understanding comes from observing all the parts together as a totality and through examining the relationship of one part to another. The one component that sustains harmony among the parts is what we call the spirit.

For readers interested in an integrated program for health, *The Holistic Way to Health and Happiness: A New Approach to Complete Lifetime Wellness*, by Harold H. Bloomfield, M.D., and Robert B. Kory, provides a sound, easy-to-understand, practical guide.

In concluding this multifaceted view of keeping fit, we should consider once again the role of humor in health maintenance. Mirth and laughter are important contributors to well-being and can be specifically employed to reduce stress and improve respiratory and cardiovascular function. A sense of humor is essential to good mental, emotional and spiritual health. Humor contributes to the buoyant spirit that energizes our total being.

As it is not proper to cure the eyes without the head, nor the head without the body, so neither is it proper to cure the body without the soul.

—SOCRATES

LIGHTEN UP

The Catch-22 is that your problem isn't funny...but laughing about it can relieve the tensions that help perpetuate it. At any rate it may be worth the experiment to see whether humor can help one to get a love handle on a hateful subject. If you can laugh at yourself about your problem, there's a chance that you'll laugh *with* yourself without your problem.

Mother Nature has always provided. By the time we reach the sitting around stage, she gives us a bigger cushion.

•

Reducing is wishful shrinking.

•

The world of show business was saddened today by the news that Luciano Pavarotti has split up.

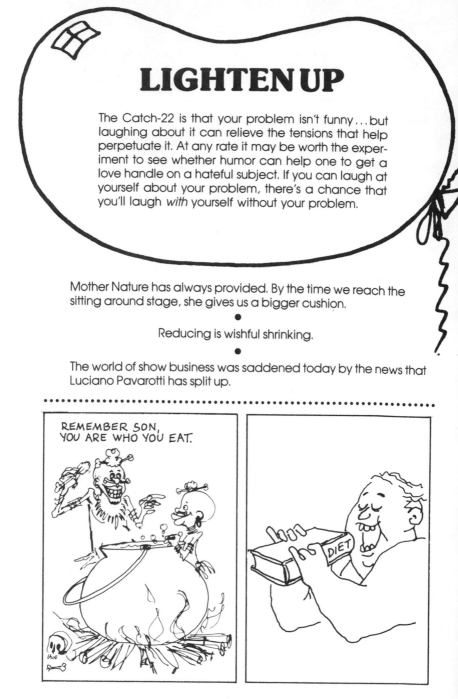

REMEMBER SON,
YOU ARE WHO YOU EAT.

DIET

SCENARIO FOR USE OF JUSTIFICATION TOOL

When those slim sages make those unflattering references to your girth and suggest you are eating too much of the wrong things and should avoid them at all cost . . . hand them the card below.

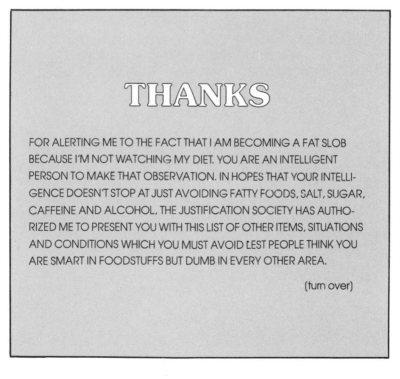

THANKS

FOR ALERTING ME TO THE FACT THAT I AM BECOMING A FAT SLOB BECAUSE I'M NOT WATCHING MY DIET. YOU ARE AN INTELLIGENT PERSON TO MAKE THAT OBSERVATION. IN HOPES THAT YOUR INTELLI-GENCE DOESN'T STOP AT JUST AVOIDING FATTY FOODS, SALT, SUGAR, CAFFEINE AND ALCOHOL, THE JUSTIFICATION SOCIETY HAS AUTHO-RIZED ME TO PRESENT YOU WITH THIS LIST OF OTHER ITEMS, SITUATIONS AND CONDITIONS WHICH YOU MUST AVOID LEST PEOPLE THINK YOU ARE SMART IN FOODSTUFFS BUT DUMB IN EVERY OTHER AREA.

(turn over)

An overweight teenager was discussing his tennis game with a friend. "When my opponent hits the ball to me, my brain immediately barks out a command to my body: 'Race up to the net,' it says. 'Slam a blistering drive to the far corner of the court, jump back into the position to return the next volley,' Then my body says, 'Who . . . me?'"

"The doctor diagnosed obesity, but I'm going to get a second opinion."

breathing • drinking water • running • jogging
dam collapse • tire • explosion • tornadoes
earthquakes • asbestos • teflon • roller skating
red dye #2 • phenesterin • swimming • hair dyes
railroad crossings • skiing • boating • rape
murder • incest • insect bites • lightning
mercury • pesticides • herbicides • cobalt
strontium 90 • isophosamide • iodine • cyclones
overturned rafts • sinking ships • poison oak
ingrown toenail • falls • drowning • influenza
newsprint • elevators • tunnels • aspirin
colored toilet paper • bathtubs • proximity to television
tubes • microwave ovens • hydrocarbons
fluorides • schoolyards • sidewalks • airplanes
buses • coal mines • freeway driving • nonfreeway
driving • paper cuts • choking • scalp infection
sharp implements • dull implements • random
violence • agent orange • detergent • dust
mugging • bores • prescription drugs
nonprescription drugs

"My doctor has advised me to give up those intimate little dinners for four, unless there are three other people eating with me."—ORSON WELLES

●

Diet warning: Taste makes waist.

●

I'm not going to starve to death just so I can live a little longer.
—IRENE PETER

●

The waist is a terrible thing to mind.

BLAZING LUNGS

When I was a kid, my mother had been trying to get my father to stop his endless chain smoking . . . he would pass it off with a remark that he didn't inhale. Later, while Mom and Dad and I were at a circus, the ringmaster introduced a daredevil who was about to leap from a one hundred foot tower into a small vat of water while lighting and smoking a cigarette in a long holder. I said I thought the guy was nuts to do such a dangerous thing. My mother said loud enough for Pop to hear, "Not really. He doesn't inhale."

Mama gave me my first example of a laughter prescription.

WOULD YOU LIKE TO DRIVE YOUR OWN $20,000 GRAN TURISMO SPORTS CAR?

WOULD YOU LIKE TO CAPTAIN YOUR OWN 150 FT. LUXURY YACHT?

WOULD YOU LIKE A 30 CARAT EMERALD CUT DIAMOND?

IF YOU ANSWERED YES, YOU'RE A LOT LIKE US.

IF YOU ANSWERED NO... THINK IT OVER.

Chinese proverb: Many man smoke, but Foo Manchu.

What this country needs is a good no-scent cigar.

Don't smoke in bed unless you want to make an ash of yourself.

As ye smoke, so shall ye reek.

DO YOU WISH A CIGARETTE?

NO, I'M TRYING TO QUIT.

THE HUMOR POTENTIAL MOVEMENT

DELIGHTENMENT
SECONDARY SCREAM
GEVALT THERAPY
EST. 1924
SANDSTONE
THE GURU MART

T'AI CHEECH CHONG
SCIENCEDOLLARGY
T AND A
WOLFING
GRINDSTONE
BABA LU

CLOTHED ENCOUNTERS • TRASCENDENTAL MEDICATION • SILVERMAN
MIND CONTROL • SWAMI SNATCHAMOOLA • THE MASHUGANISHI • ZEST

THE L.A.U.G.H. TELETHON
(A PUBLIC SERVICE ANNOUNCEMENT)

Watch for the 5 danger signals of the nation's number one killer:

1. Breathing.
2. A persistent pulsing sound in chest.
3. Recurring experiences of daylight followed by intervals of darkness.
4. Excitement and boredom.
5. Shortness of cash.

Any of these signs may indicate that you've come down with a case of LIFE.

Don't be alarmed. There is no known cure, but there is hope. Hope that the pain of LIFE can be lessened by appropriate treatments of Humor therapy.

The LIFE ASSOCIATION for the USE of GOOD HUMOR once again asks you to support the L.A.U.G.H. TELETHON. Give till it helps.

Do it for God and his kids.

Tonight . . . right after S.O.A.P. (the Stamp Out Acronyms Program).

"I'm really looking forward to an intensive learning experience at the center. I'm going to take Burmese acupuncture, energy balance and control, rejuvenation of the body and control of the psychic centers, Western Tantric and Caucasian Yoga, Sufi Breath of Liberation, Moon Cycles, Kundalini Massage, psychokinesis, Auric color therapy and psychic karate. Then, after lunch . . .

From the SAFFRON PAGES:
In a hurry for enlightenment?
Call Awareness Delight . . .
We Deliver

REPORTER: I understand you've just hired a press agent to publicize your teachings.

SWAMI: Yes, that is correct. This press agent has just been assigned to distribute my precepts to the four corners of the earth. He claims he can spread my message with great speed.

REPORTER: Could you share some of these precepts with us?

SWAMI: I would be delighted: "A stitch in time saves nine"; "A bird in the hand is worth two in the bush"; and "A penny saved is a penny earned."

REPORTER: Those are very familiar sayings already.

SWAMI: I told you he worked fast!

A Zen Master was approached by a disciple seeking enlightenment. The Zen Master asked the disciple to build him a temple. The disciple did so, but the Master was displeased and told the disciple to tear it down and build another one. The disciple did as he was told, but the Zen Master didn't like the second temple and instructed the disciple to build a third one. This happened twenty times. The disciple building, the Master being displeased and the disciple tearing down the temple. Finally, when the disciple had finished the twenty-first temple and the Zen Master said "Tear it down," the disciple said "Up yours, Master."

"Now, you are enlightened," said the Master.

FRAGMENT OF CONVERSATION AT ASHRAM

DEVOTEE: Tell me more about your austere life.

TEACHER: Some time ago I divested myself of all my worldly goods.

DEVOTEE: Then how do you account for these fabulous surroundings and the Ferrari, Rolls and Mercedes?

TEACHER: Oh, those are my worldly bads. I just ditched my worldly goods . . . the hair shirt, nail mattress . . . it's a sacrifice, but, anything for my followers.

GURU UNIVERSITY EXTENSION COURSES

Choice as a Way of Life. Demonstrates how when one has the choice between sick and poor and rich and healthy, rich and healthy is the way to go.

Failure. A Way of Life. S. M. Handelman, Prof. How people who are successes are really just expressing nonfailure.

Basic Blaming. Denies the theory of taking responsibility for your lot in life. Helps you isolate those to blame and suggests appropriate action.

Keeping It. Discourses on possessiveness and how attempts to hold on to an antipossessiveness attitude is just another form of possessiveness.

Transcendental Medication. Course includes samplings of lysergic acid diethylamide, dimethyl triptamine, tetrahydracannibinol and psilocbye mexicana. Passport photo required.

Blasting In. Inner space travel explored. Why ingestion of psychoactive or psychomemetic substances of a hallucinogenic nature is counterproductive to achieving experiences of a transpersonal nature while attaining transcendant states of consciousness is o.k.

The Pyramid and You. How the pyramid can be used creatively to dramatically transform you to another level not by sitting *in* it but by sitting *on* it.

I'VE MASTERED MEDITATION. I'M JUST HUMMING ALONG. I FEEL COMPLETELY BALANCED, CENTERED, ALIGNED AND ENERGIZED.

IS THIS FROM MEDITATION OR DID YOU GET YOURSELF A LUBE JOB?

HUMOR POTENTIAL COURSE

ESS—Edible Seminar Sessions From the German *essen*, to eat, ESS derives from man's capacity to devour his troubles, digest them, and expel or evacuate them just in the process of eating himself.

THE PSYCHOMAT

A chain of fast food for thought franchises.

●

My dad believed in meditation . . . he used to tell me "Sit down and shut up!"

●

If it wasn't for half the people in the world, the other half would be all of them.

—COLONEL STOPNAGEL

3.
Health Makes Wealth

●●●

The first wealth is health.
Sickness is poor-spirited,
and cannot serve anyone.
—RALPH WALDO EMERSON

There is an old saying that makes a lot of sense, "Health Makes Wealth"—but it doesn't work the other way around. Even if health is not essential to success, success without health is a hollow victory. Health alone can be a source of joy and satisfaction. When we consider the great amounts of money being spent in attempts to obtain joy and satisfaction, we must conclude that health is wealth.

> *The poorest man would not part with health for money, but the richest would gladly part with all his money for health.*
>
> —C.C. COLTON

Now that the relationship between humor and health has been well established, let's look at the relationship between humor and success.

The premise of this book is that humor is a form of energy that can be channeled to achieve desired goals. Humor can be directed into the success channel. Success is getting what you want; happiness is wanting what you get.

It is not my intention to define wealth narrowly. The word

means many things. Wealth can be a profusion of money or material possessions and can also be an abundance of health, satisfaction or happiness.

I've never been poor, only broke. Being poor is a frame of mind. Being broke is only a temporary situation.
—MIKE TODD

Material wealth can be inherited, or created by others, but accomplishment and satisfaction must be achieved by the individual. Personal success cannot be measured by accomplishment alone. It is a combination of achievement and satisfaction.

No matter where you are socially or economically, humor can help you succeed. It won't solve your financial problems or make you lovable and popular, but it can help you see your financial problems in perspective and be the social lubricant that warms up your personal relationships.

No matter what your occupation—doctor, lawyer, merchant, mailman—and no matter what level you occupy in the hierarchy, the energy of humor can enhance your job. It can improve communication, motivate others and help solve difficult problems.

•••

NEVER TOO YOUNG TO LEARN

UPI reported the following medical techniques derived from a first aid test by a fourth-grade class in Edmonds, Washington:

For head colds, "Use an agonizer to spray the nose until it drops in the throat."

For nosebleed, "Put the nose lower than the body."

For snakebite, "Bleed the wound and rape the victim in a blanket for shock."

For fractures, "To see if the limb is broken, wiggle it gently back and forth."

For fainting, "Rub the person's chest, or if it is a lady, rub her arm above the hand."

For asphyxiation, "Apply artificial respiration until the victim's dead."

MORAL: Don't ever require first aid while on or near an elementary schoolground.

•••

Humor is just another defense against the universe.
—MEL BROOKS

When talking with your co-workers or others in the same job or profession, humor that is related to your work can provide the common ground for effective communication. Politics, religion and taste may be conflicting, but when you share laughter about your work you may find that you have experiences and goals in common. Jokes and humorous anecdotes about your profession improve interaction within your peer group and create an environment in which feelings can be communicated and exchanged.

In the business world an executive knows something about everything, a technician knows everything about something—and the switchboard operator knows everything.
—HAROLD COFFIN

By laughing at yourself, you can avoid creating the impression of being pompous or too self-important. Make jokes about yourself. Tell humorous stories about your own mistakes. Accept compliments or awards with a smile or witty remarks as though you are surprised that anyone would think you were outstanding. This approach will generate more good feelings and respect than a solemn one.

It dawned on me then that as long as I could laugh, I was safe from the world; and I have learned since that laughter keeps me safe from myself, too. All of us have schnozzles—are ridiculous in one way or another, if not in our faces, then in our characters, minds or habits. When we admit our schnozzles, instead of defending them, we begin to laugh, and the world laughs with us.
—JIMMY DURANTE

In a recent survey about humor, the majority of respondents volunteered that they liked to be around people who had a good sense of humor and people who laughed easily. This response is of particular interest, because they were asked only, "What makes you laugh?" The fact that people like to be with others who have a good sense of humor means that a sense of humor is a real asset in just about any line of work.

Health and humor are important to professional success. Humor can be applied effectively to enhance every aspect of life, though few have explored its practical benefits. Perhaps it has much more to offer if you give it a little more concentrated attention.

Laugh at yourself first, before anyone else can.
> —ELSA MAXWELL

Many fear that too much investigation of humor will destroy their capacity to enjoy it. There is no evidence to support this point of view. The psychologists, medical researchers, sociologists and others who study humor have not lost their senses of humor. My own experience and observation suggests that their senses of humor have been heightened by learning more about the subject. Gaining new knowledge about the nature and uses of humor and its application to life's problems is a safe venture. There is no other activity that can be as rewarding in so many areas of your life.

JOSÉ SUPERSPORT

José Jimenez, the comedy invention of my co-author, Bill Dana, is a good example of the use of humor in physical fitness and the sporting life. Here is a transcript of my conversation with Mr. Jimenez on the subject.

—LAURENCE PETER

LP: *What is the place of food in your regime?*
JOSÉ: Mostly in my stomach...but sometimes on my lap.
LP: *I mean, is diet important to you?*
JOSÉ: I feel diet is important to anyone who wants to be physically fit. Otherwise, you get physically fat.
LP: *You've been a baseball player, a football player, a skier, a surfer, a track star, a hockey player... what else have you been?*

JOSÉ: Exhausted.
LP: *We'd be interested in hearing about your career as a surfer.*
JOSÉ: That's a good tie-in with my desire to talk about it. You know I am called The King of Surf.
LP: *How did you become King of Surf?*
JOSÉ: I had cards printed.
LP: *Besides being great exercise, surfing is quite romantic, isn't it?*
JOSÉ: Oh, yes. One time we actually had a wedding of two surfers on surfboards. They met on a surf-

board, they got engaged on a surfboard, they got married on a surfboard. Then it got a little tricky.

LP: *Switching from the beach to the mountains, tell us about your Olympic skiing exploits.*

JOSÉ: I was in the giant slalom at Mount Blanc where you dash down the hill narrowly missing the sharp poles; I was in the bobsled events where I raced on the dangerous icy track; I was in the treacherous ski jump where you jump from hundreds of feet in the air onto the hard snow below.

LP: *What else were you in?*

JOSÉ: Traction. I went from Mount Blanc to Mount Sinai.

LP: *As a track star, weren't you expert with the javelin?*

JOSÉ: I'm one of the few to ever throw a javelin two hundred yards.

LP: *Two hundred yards...that's amazing.*

JOSÉ: Well, actually, I only threw it one hundred yards, the guy it hit crawled the other hundred.

LP: *As a baseball player, what is your favorite position?*

JOSÉ: Sort of curled up like this with my blanket in my hand. I was a bonus baby.

LP: *I mean, I heard you were quite a pitcher.*

JOSÉ: That's right. I could throw a fast ball, a slow ball, a curve and a knuckle ball.

LP: *When you face a powerful hitter like Reggie Jackson, what do you throw?*

JOSÉ: I throw up.

LP: *What about football?*

JOSÉ: It's a thing made from a pig that looks like a little Goodrich blimp.

LP: *I mean, what was your most memorable moment as a football player?*

JOSÉ: One time I got the ball behind the goalpost and started to run and they tried to tackle me but they couldn't stop me so they took out knives and that didn't work and I kept on running and they shot pistols and rifles at me and then came the tanks and that didn't stop me so the airplanes swooped down and shot me with machine guns and...

LP: *Excuse me, José...but this is ridiculous. Anybody that was in the stands that day can prove you are a liar.*

JOSÉ: There were no survivors.

4
Peter's Pharmacy

●●

Discover the Secrets of Health and Happiness

1. Learn a new health science through home study.
2. Gain expert knowledge about humor and health.
3. Learn why humor is your best medicine.
4. Help yourself and others by becoming a humor therapist.

BOOKS

The Peter Principle: Why Things Always Go Wrong. Dr. Laurence J. Peter and Raymond Hull. William Morrow and Company, Inc., New York, 1969.

The authors explain why the human race is foundering in a morass of occupational, academic and administrative inefficiency. The book not only reveals why the world is so completely screwed up, but also provides proven techniques for creative control of personal, social and business problems. It analyzes the reasons for human failure and tells how to achieve a state of well-being by avoiding mindless escalation to your level of incompetence. The book is written as deadpan satire.

Anatomy of an Illness, As Perceived by the Patient: Reflections on Healing and Regeneration, Norman Cousins, W.W. Norton and Company, New York, 1979.

This is a case study of one patient's recovery from a crippling and supposedly irreversible disease. It tells of the partnership drawn up between physician and patient to mobilize the patient's own capabilities for healing. Mr. Cousins writes convincingly of the values of hope, confidence and laughter not only as therapy but in the enhancement of everyday life. Formerly editor of *Saturday Review* magazine for more than thirty years, Mr. Cousins is now adjunct professor in the School of Medicine, University of California at Los Angeles, and consulting editor of *Man and Medicine*, published at the College of Physicians and Surgeons, Columbia University.

A Surgeon's Book of Hope, Dr. William A. Nolen. Coward, McCann and Geoghegan, New York, 1980.

In this book, Dr. Nolen has collected twenty-two case histories that are reason for hope even in what appear to be dire medical circumstances. The book is informative, reassuring and inspiring.

Laugh after Laugh: The Healing Power of Humor, Raymond A. Moody, Jr., M.D. Headwaters Press, Staunton, Virginia, 1978.

The author describes the process of healing by humor as well as the problems that can result from ridicule and other negative uses of humor. He discusses laughter that results from neurological disease, such as pseudobulbar palsy, amytropic lateral sclerosis and multiple sclerosis. Dr. Moody also discusses pathological laughter that accompanies certain psychotic conditions. He brings together a historical perspective, contemporary research and suggestions for the use of humor in medical practice.

Can be obtained through Headwaters Press, P.O. Box 727, Staunton, Virginia 24401.

The Pritikin Program for Diet and Exercise, Nathan Pritikin with Patrick M. Grady, Jr., Bantam Books, New York, 1979.

The authors of this well-written bestseller describe the complete Pritikin Program as developed at the famous Longevity and Pritikin Research Foundation. They provide detailed instructions, and the book includes a cookbook, so the reader can learn everything needed to make the diet-exercise health plan work. A weight loss and maintenance program for a longer, healthier life are included as well.

Human Life Styling: Keeping Whole in the 20th Century, John C. McCamy, M.D., and James Presley, Harper and Row, New York, 1975.

The major thrust of this book is the delineation of a life style that prevents disease. It is a synthesis of the known techniques of disease prevention and a guide to improving one's life both in the present and for a happier, healthier future. Based on the premise that you are what you eat, drink, breathe, think and do, the program offers a synergistic plan that shows how to make the body and mind work together for a stronger, better-functioning you with increased resistance to stress and decreased susceptibility to disease.

The Holistic Way to Health and Happiness: A New Approach to Complete Lifetime Wellness, Harold H. Bloomfield, M.D., and Robert B. Kory. Simon & Schuster, New York, 1978.

Dr. Bloomfield, one of the founders of holistic medical treatment, shows how you can acquire your full measure of health and vitality through taking advantage of your own natural healing abilities. The book provides strategies for dealing with smoking, overweightness, high blood pressure, insomnia, stress and heart disease. The authors avoid complicated technical language and present a complex subject in a style that is a pleasure to read.

AUDIO TAPES

Cassette tapes containing self-instructional and self-help information provide a convenient means for many persons to learn how to improve their health. One of the advantages of the taped message over a book is that it can be listened to while performing routine tasks, exercising or driving or riding to work. Some are readings of well-known books, while others are lectures and instructions by experts.

What Is Good Health? Dr. John L. Boyer. Write: Spenco Medical Corporation, P.O. Box 8113, Waco, Texas 76710.

Dr. John L. Boyer, medical director of the Exercise and Adult Fitness Center at San Diego State University, describes how good health is not simply the absence of disease but a condition of positive well-being. It involves having energy and vigor to work and play and live life fully. Dr. Boyer discusses health issues in a manner that is understandable and applicable to lay listeners.

How to Live 365 Days a Year, Dr. John A. Schindler. Write: Success Motivation Institute, P.O. Box 7614, Waco, Texas 76710.

Dr. John A. Schindler's message is that we should make every day

count. Lost time is the only possession that can't be replaced. When you merely exist part of your days, your life is actually cut short by that length of time. Follow his suggestions and learn how to get more out of life.

Listen and Lose, Dr. Robert Parrish. Write: Success Motivation Institute, P.O. Box 7614, Waco, Texas 76710.

Dr. Robert Parrish employs a psychological approach to help listeners lose weight. This approach involves visualizing being slim. He believes that without this use of the unconscious mind, any diet will fail. The tape is designed to help you achieve this slim image.

Running, Barry Konicov. Write: Potentials Unlimited, 9390 Whitneyville Road, Alto, Michigan 49508.

Barry Konicov, a hypnotist, provides self-hypnosis instruction to help the listener acquire a positive attitude toward running as an exercise. The objective is for you to gain mental control of the release of ketone—a body chemical that produces the euphoric state, or high, achieved by runners—in less time and with less effort.

New Approaches to Headache Management, Dr. Seymour Diamond, et al. Write: BMA Audio Cassettes, 200 Park Avenue South, New York, New York 10003.

Seymour Diamond and other physicians discuss their experiences with feedback in the treatment of headaches and compare the value of feedback with that of other treatments and procedures for this common disorder.

PART II

Coping with Stress

Relax and Be Happy

5.

Reducing Anxiety

*I've developed a new
philosophy... I only dread
one day at a time.*

—CHARLIE BROWN

Worry and anxiety are the most widespread causes of distress today. According to the Food and Drug Administration (FDA), the drugs prescribed most in America are tranquilizers, and the most widely used nonprescriptive drug is aspirin. Those of us who worry are not alone.

> *One out of four people in this country is mentally imbalanced. Think of your three closest friends. If they seem okay, then you're the one.*
>
> —ANN LANDERS

In this chapter, we will describe three self-help approaches for reducing anxiety that involve neither medication nor psychotherapy: (1) Enhanced life style, (2) Relaxation and (3) Laughter.

LIFE STYLE

Life would be very dull if we did not get excited about things. The emotions aroused by beauty, competition and anticipation are the spices of life. The arousal experienced during sex, eating, athletic competition or any enjoyable activity are physiological states of stress. When one feels excited about a new discovery, or feels anything strongly—whether it is fear, anger, desire or love —one is experiencing stress. It is stress that mobilizes our energies for activity, achievement and peak performance. Stress is not only desirable but is essential to life. We should not eliminate stress; rather, we should learn to control the anxieties that dissipate our energies by nonproductive worrying. In his book *Stress without Distress*, Dr. Hans Selye, the foremost authority on stress, makes a distinction between stress that is energizing and distress that is debilitating: "Stress is the spice of life.... Complete freedom from stress is death."

Stress, says Dr. Selye, is the nonspecific response of the body to any demand made upon it. It is immaterial whether the situation we face is pleasant or unpleasant. All that counts is the intensity of the demand for readjustment or adaptation. Any arousal state produces a physiological imbalance—an internal demand for homeostasis, or balance. Since the body's store of adaptive energy required to restore this balance is limited, it is not capable of accommodating unlimited stress.

We worry because there is a lot to worry about. We all live in a high-risk neighborhood—the world. The energy crisis will be with us for a long time. Violence is on the increase. Inflation is out of control. As if this were not enough, we have personal concerns—our health, our children, old age, death and taxes. Will we have an accident with our car? Will the plane crash? Will our savings disappear?

> *Worry is interest paid on trouble before it falls due.*
> —DEAN INGE

For everyone, rich or poor, strong or weak, life is full of uncertainties. Before you get too involved in worrying about that fact, ask yourself these questions: (1) Will worry or anxiety reduce the amount of illness? (2) Will worry save me money? and (3) Will worry help me avoid an automobile accident?

Worry will erode your health, make you accident-prone and hasten your trip to the point of no return. It is more likely to stop you from taking constructive action about your problems. Worry is a self-destructive activity. Arousal or stress that leads to constructive action may improve your health, make you a more alert driver or a more sensitive and effective parent. The choice is yours: Either be assured of failure by fearing the future, or risk failure and forge ahead, enjoying yourself while facing life's uncertainties.

Not everything that is faced can be changed, but nothing can be changed until it is faced.

—JAMES BALDWIN

The better adjusted you are and the more satisfying your life style, the more readily you will respond to the humor in jokes, cartoons and everyday situations. People with an unsatisfying life style, those who are maladjusted, tend to miss the point in a joke, funny remark or humorous situation. The ability to get a laugh out of everyday situations is a safety valve that will rid you of tensions that might otherwise continue to build and damage your health.

A person without a sense of humor is like a wagon without springs—jolted by every pebble in the road.

—HENRY WARD BEECHER

The life of the well-adjusted individual consists of waves of arousal followed by dissipation of the stress and recovery of the body's homeostasis. When stress is not dissipated through this natural rhythm, it can be reduced by taking drugs or alcohol. These produce temporary relief but frequently have harmful long-term results because of adverse side effects, particularly addiction. The problems of living that interfere with the natural cycle of arousal and relaxation are not resolved by the use of drugs and alcohol.

Our jobs and responsibilities frequently require continual or intermittent coping with stress. The routines of daily living— such as driving a car, shopping, dealing with government and private agencies—all can produce distress and psychological pain. Living with and relating to others, no matter how much we care for them, creates conflicts, misunderstandings and pent-up aggressive impulses. Because we have social consciences and are concerned for others, we must at times curb aggressive impulses and repress expression of our emotional distress. Furthermore, society only accepts direct expression of these feelings under limited circumstances, such as in therapeutic or counseling sessions. Since it is unhealthy to repress and build up feelings of distress, and since we are not going to seek a therapist every day just so we can express our accumulation of stress and hostile impulses, we must learn to express them in socially acceptable ways. Wit, humor and a satirical view of life and its problems serve precisely this function.

Humor is not only socially acceptable, it is actually welcomed. Healthy adjustment includes both the ability to control expression of feelings when inappropriate and to express feelings when the time is right.

> **Anybody who goes to see a psychiatrist ought to have his head examined.**
>
> **—SAMUEL GOLDWYN**

We need periodic release from the obligation to be logical and serious about life's responsibilities. Humor allows us to deal in fantasy and nonsense and find respite from our serious cares and responsibilities.

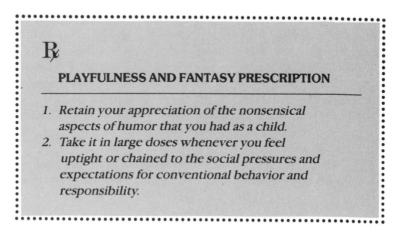

℞

PLAYFULNESS AND FANTASY PRESCRIPTION

1. *Retain your appreciation of the nonsensical aspects of humor that you had as a child.*
2. *Take it in large doses whenever you feel uptight or chained to the social pressures and expectations for conventional behavior and responsibility.*

Having a sense of humor does not mean that you go around laughing at everything. It does mean that you see the funny side along with the serious side. The humorous approach to life is held by persons of both a quiet and a boisterous nature.

RELAXATION

The ability to relax can protect us from the health hazards of excessive stress. If we can divide problems into those that can be solved and those that cannot, we will have come a long way toward relaxing when confronted with things we can't change. By engaging in a sport or some vigorous physical activity, we can work off those tensions that build up during the day.

> *The only difference between a rut and a grave is their dimensions.*
>
> —ELLEN GLASGOW

We have seen that worrying is a self-destructive mental activity. It produces a physiological condition—including such symptoms as rapid heart beat, accelerated breathing, increased muscle tension, perspiration and high levels of stress hormones in the blood—which, in turn, produces unpleasant feelings, including apprehension, irritability and painful tension. Breaking this cycle of worry or anxiety is often difficult.

> *The longer we dwell on our misfortunes, the greater is their power to harm us.*
>
> —VOLTAIRE

In this complex cycle—in which mind, muscles, stress hormones and electrical activity of the brain and nervous system play a part—release of tension can be achieved through intervention at any point. Here are three examples: (1) Tranquilizers, such as Valium, Librium or alcohol, produce physical changes that cause anxiety to subside. As I've said, these methods only bring temporary relief and can be harmful. (2) Positive changes in thought or mental attitude produce physiological changes, including reduction of stress hormones. (3) Reduction of muscle tension inhibits mental anxiety and lessens emotional stress.

Dr. Herbert Benson, in his book *The Relaxation Response*, describes a simple meditative technique that has been studied scientifically and has been proven to be effective in reducing stress. The Benson method is a combination and simplification of ancient and modern relaxation techniques. The book provides straightforward instructions, so that the reader can master the technique without the help of a personal instructor. The four essential requirements to relaxation are outlined in the following prescription.*

R

BENSON'S RELAXATION RESPONSE PRESCRIPTIONS

1. A Quiet Environment. *Choose a quiet, calm place with as few distractions as possible. Deeply relax all your muscles, beginning at your feet and progressing up to your face.*
2. A Mental Device. *To shift the mind from externally oriented thought requires a constant stimulus, such as a silently spoken repeated word or phrase. Breathe through your nose and become aware of your breathing. As you breathe out, say the word, "one" silently to yourself.*
3. A Passive Attitude. *When distracting thoughts occur, they are to be disregarded and attention redirected to the breathing and repetition of the word "one." You should not worry about how well you are doing. Adopt a let-it-happen attitude.*
4. A Comfortable Position. *The relaxation, breathing and repetition of the word "one" should all occur while you are in a comfortable position, so there is no undue muscle tension. Sitting quietly is satisfactory for most individuals.*

Ten or twenty minutes of the Benson method should bring about significant relaxation. Practiced daily, it has been shown to be effective in reducing chronic tension and high blood pressure.

Psychologist Dr. Alfred A. Bach uses an easy-to-learn technique in teaching ways to release tension.

---

*This brief description is not intended to be a substitute for careful study of all the details of the technique.

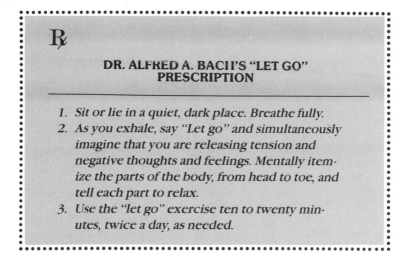

R̥

DR. ALFRED A. BACH'S "LET GO" PRESCRIPTION

1. Sit or lie in a quiet, dark place. Breathe fully.
2. As you exhale, say "Let go" and simultaneously imagine that you are releasing tension and negative thoughts and feelings. Mentally itemize the parts of the body, from head to toe, and tell each part to relax.
3. Use the "let go" exercise ten to twenty minutes, twice a day, as needed.

Reason and sense remove anxiety, not villas that look out upon the sea.

—HORACE

LAUGHTER

Laughter has an effective and specific role to play in reducing tension. When an individual succumbs to a fit of laughter, he or she becomes physically limp. In the case of extended spells of laughter, an individual may have to sit down, for fear of falling, or may literally "fall down laughing." This is caused by a loss of tension in the skeletal muscles. Laughter of less intensity produces a relatively smaller muscle relaxation. Immediately following laughter, it is a common experience to find a loss of muscle tone to the degree that makes it difficult or impossible to write, thread a needle or perform other tasks requiring fine muscle coordination.

The relaxation response to laughter has been studied scientifically. The sensation begins with an anticipatory response, when the individual perceives that something is potentially funny. In the hearing of a joke, the listener anticipates that there will be something funny, and as he or she listens to the buildup, there is a short-term increase in arousal, or stress. This has been measured as increased pulse, peripheral skin temperature and blood pressure. As the laughter begins to subside after the punchline, this short-term effect begins to decrease. Tension continues to decrease until it is substantially lower than before the humor stimulus began. This decrease may continue for some time and has been measured as lasting up to forty-five minutes. The greater the intensity of the laughter, the larger the decrease in tension and the more long-lasting the effect.

> *Strange when you come to think of it, that of all the countless folk who have lived before our time on the planet, not one is known in history or in legend as having died of laughter.*
>
> —SIR MAX BEERBOHM

Laughter's ability to cause the muscles to go suddenly limp is of great value in the treatment of stress. It is difficult to be anxious when the muscles are in a state of deep relaxation; muscle relaxation and anxiety are incompatible.

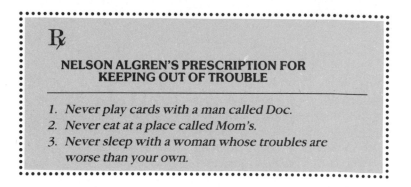

℞

NELSON ALGREN'S PRESCRIPTION FOR KEEPING OUT OF TROUBLE

1. *Never play cards with a man called Doc.*
2. *Never eat at a place called Mom's.*
3. *Never sleep with a woman whose troubles are worse than your own.*

Stress reduction through laughter contributes not only to physical well-being but to finding the cause of emotional problems, because an individual is able to explore his/her sources of distress.

In conclusion, a sense of humor and a life style that avoids buildup of anxiety will help protect you from the distress that emotional tension may bring on. When you do suffer from tension there are three nonmedical things you can do: (1) You can try meditative relaxation. (2) You can engage in vigorous activity, such as swimming, running or tennis. (3) You can laugh.

DOES IT HURT CORPORAL?

ONLY WHEN I
LAUGH SIR!

· ·

YOU CALL THIS A RANCH?
WHY I COULD GET INTO MY CAR,
START EARLY IN THE MORNING
AND STILL NOT HAVE REACHED
THE END OF MY SPREAD
BY SUNDOWN.

I HAD A CAR
LIKE THAT
ONCE.

JOSÉ JIMENEZ... USES THE PRESCRIPTIONS OF LAUGHTER

José Jimenez provides a good example of using humor to cope with adversity. The tribulations of assimilation in a foreign society, the fears of acquitting himself in his mythical dangerous professions, his devotion to self-improvement of mind and body all make this quixotic character worth listening to. Here are some transcripts of my conversations with Mr. Jimenez in his various roles.

—LAURENCE PETER

JOSÉ THE ASTRONAUT

LP: I see you have some of your space equipment with you. What is that called, a crash helmet?
JOSÉ: I hope not.
LP: What do you consider the most important part of space travel?
JOSÉ: The most important part of space travel is the blast-off.
LP: The blast-off?
JOSÉ: Yes. I always take a blast before I take off. Otherwise I wouldn't go near that thing.
LP: Sir, Gordon Cooper of Project Mercury called his space capsule Faith Seven. What do you call yours?
JOSÉ: I call my capsule Hope and Charity.
LP: Why is that?
JOSÉ: 'Cause I got no faith in it. But I like what the Russians call their capsule. The first one they sent up was a Sputnik and then they sent up a dog and they called it a Mutnik. And now they

are going to send up a man and a woman together in the same capsule.
LP: And what will that be called?
JOSÉ: A Picnic. If they work it right it really could be fun and games in the weightless state.
LP: Speaking of Russians, while you were in orbit, did you pass the Russian capsule?
JOSÉ: I didn't even swallow it.

LP: Let's change the subject. How do you plan to entertain yourself on that long, lonesome, solitary voyage all by yourself?
JOSÉ: I plan to cry a lot. I could start right now if you want.
LP: No, no, that won't be necessary, sir. When you get back to earth where will you be landing?
JOSÉ: I am going to be landing in Nevada.
LP: The state of Nevada?
JOSÉ: The state of Nevada.
LP: Then you are convinced they will bring you back to earth?
JOSÉ: I am convinced they will bring me back to earth. Just how far into it—that's what I'm not convinced about.
LP: But surely they have made some provisions for breaking your fall?
JOSÉ: The state of Nevada—that would break anybody.
LP: I must say, sir, you are to be congratulated on this dangerous undertaking.
JOSÉ: Don't say undertaking.
LP: Oh, forgive me, dangerous mission.

JOSÉ: That's a better choice of words.
LP: One last question before you leave the rostrum.
JOSÉ: I don't have to go to the restroom.
LP: One last thing before you go.
JOSÉ: I said I don't have to go.
LP: Mr. Jimenez.
JOSÉ: Don't force me to go.
LP: I'm not. I'm not, sir.
JOSÉ: That could really hurt a person you know.
LP: Yes, I know. You don't understand, Mr. Jimenez. You see, this is the rostrum right here. This is the rostrum.
JOSÉ: You're kidding.
LP: No, this is the rostrum.
JOSÉ: I dare you.
LP: I beg your pardon?
JOSÉ: I mean where could you write your name?
LP: Sir, is there anything you'd like to say to the people of America before you leave on this most perilous mission?
JOSÉ: Yes. There is. People of America. Please don't let them do this to me!

JOSÉ THE DEEP SEA DIVER

LP: Where do you do most of your diving?
JOSÉ: I do most of my diving in the water.
LP: I see.
JOSÉ: I can, too, but it's murky.

LP: Didn't you start out in the submarine service?

JOSÉ: Yes. I was on the first atomic sub to go around the world underwater in eighty-four days.

LP: In that time, did you have any trouble?

JOSÉ: We had trouble with the system that lets you come back up to the surface.

LP: How long did it take you to fix it?

JOSÉ: Eighty-three days. You don't think we were down there on purpose, do you?

LP: Eighty-three days with all those men jammed together. Was there ever any trouble with irritability from the confinement?

JOSÉ: Just once we had a little trouble.

LP: When was that?

JOSÉ: During the third riot.

LP: What was the most frightening experience you ever had?

JOSÉ: Once when I was diving at low feet, we got a message from the captain up on top of the water that scared the devil out of us.

LP: What did he say?

JOSÉ: Come on up, the boat is sinking.

JOSÉ THE MATADOR

Of all the emotions which zap our strength, fear is in the top ten. Thinking that it can benefit us to communicate with those who have fear as a constant companion, we managed to get a rare interview with José just before his entry into the famed corrida of Madrid.

LP: We realize that you don't have much time to answer questions since you must go into the ring to face the moment of truth —death in the afternoon.

JOSÉ: Take all the time you want.

LP: What was the largest bull you ever faced?

JOSÉ: Would you believe it, the largest bull I ever faced weighed three tons, five ounces.

LP: That's a lot of bull.

JOSÉ: I thought you wouldn't believe it. That's my moment of false.

LP: In bullfighting, what is your most important equipment?

JOSÉ: In bullfighting, the most

important equipment is the track shoes.

LP: Track shoes???

JOSÉ: That's right. Track shoes. Once I made it from the middle of the ring to the nearest exit in 9.5 seconds.

LP: That sounds like a record.

JOSÉ: No, the bull made it in 9.4.

LP: How do you prepare for the fight?

JOSÉ: First I go out and milk the bull.

LP: Sir, one doesn't milk a bull, one milks a cow.

JOSÉ: Let Juan fight what he wants, and I'll fight what I want.

LP: Where do you raise your bulls?

JOSÉ: I raise them on my own ranch and bring them into the ring in a little cart which I made myself. It's called a Bull Buggy.

LP: How do you make a Bull Buggy?

JOSÉ: You tickle his toes. That's a little joke around the bull ring.

LP: It didn't get any bigger here. What is the name of your ranch?

JOSÉ: The name of my ranch is the Bar Nine Circle Z Rocking Q

Four Happy Valley H Crazy Triangle Rancho Alegre.

LP: Do you have many cattle?

JOSÉ: No. Not many survived the branding. Talk about screaming bulls. That was one heck of a Bullbecue.

LP: We understand that for doing well the judges award you parts of the bull.

JOSÉ: I am happy to say that in my career I have won eight ears, seven tails and five hooves.

LP: If you'll forgive us, most matadors win more than that in a career

JOSÉ: From the same bull?

LP: Let's skip the subject.

JOSÉ: Good. I can use the exercise.

LP: Often, when I see you leap into the ring to face a ferocious bull I wonder what you are thinking.

JOSÉ: I wonder who pushed me.

LP: In conclusion. Where would you rank yourself in the bullfighters' list of greats?

JOSÉ: Oh, I'd say I am number three.

LP: Who would you rank ahead of you?

JOSÉ: Ahead of me would be George Washington and Benjamin Franklin.

LP: If you'll forgive me, Washington and Franklin were not bullfighters.

JOSÉ: My God! I'm number one!!

THE HOW-TO BOOK FOR THE 80'S

CHALLENGING TIMES

FIRST TIME EVER IN PAUPER BACK

This is the one you've been hearing about. It's got the answers to your survival questions.

HERE'S A SAMPLE OF THE CHAPTERS:

Have Money to Burn: Your lifetime savings can keep you warm.

Beggars Can Be Choosers: How to select a good corner. In begging, the three rules are Location! Location! Location!

Eat Yourself Out of House And Home: Why Not? Food is a household word. Your home ... if you can't afford to heat it, you might as well eat it. How to tenderize shingles. Not many calories in a carpet. Eat all you want! Socks as snacks. How to make soy sauce from shoe polish.

Mock Marshmallows: Don't waste that burning neighborhood! 1,001 uses for free fire.

Going to the Dogs? The Compleat Canine Cookbook: How to make Cocker Cutlets ... Scottie Scaloppine ... Chow Mein—from real Chows ... St. Bernard in its own brandy.

101 Vacation Ideas for the '80s: How to turn that spare closet into Hawaii.

How to Fight Inflation on $5,000 a Day

What to Grow in Your Defeat Garden

How to Trade Food Stamps for Weapons

Starvation: A weight-loss plan that works!

Ten Terrific Pacts with the Devil: How to sell your soul for a decent meal.

How to Bathe in a Water Cannon —and get your laundry done, too.

Be Top Dog: How to sit up and beg for rich people.

You Don't Have to Go for Broke: You're already there. Finding joy in bankruptcy.

How to Be Hard Up, Down and five other directions.

HOW TO STRETCH YOUR DOLLAR

AND OTHER *Legal* TENDER THOUGHTS

6.

Overcoming Depression

••

*It is much easier to do and die
than it is to reason why.*
—G.A. STUDDERT-KENNEDY

According to the National Institute of Mental Health, each year about fifteen million Americans suffer depression that is severe enough to be classified as medically significant—to say nothing about the minor depressions that trouble almost everyone from time to time. The severity of depression varies from the blues, which might last for a few days, to a deep, debilitating loss of interest in everything that could last for years. Severe depression should be diagnosed and treated by medical doctors, psychiatrists or psychologists. Depression, which used to be one of the most difficult emotional ills to treat, now is treated with new methods of psychotherapy and antidepressant drugs. This chapter will deal only with moderate depression—the kind that you can learn to overcome without professional help.

Moderate depression varies in intensity from a vague awareness that you are unhappy to a condition where you feel chronically tired, lack interest in everyday activities and are generally pessimistic. It is usually accompanied by a decrease in vitality, difficulty in concentrating and an inability to make decisions. Other symptoms can include irritability, in which trivial matters cause serious upsets or temper outbursts; decrease in sexual interest—even impotence; feelings of guilt and self-recrimination; a change in sleeping pattern; loss of interest in personal hygiene and appearance; excessive drinking; headaches.

The lack of humor and laughter in an individual who normally displays a sense of humor is an indicator of depression. Playfulness and depression are incompatible states of mind. Because playfulness is a prerequisite for humor, the amount of laughter and joking shown by an individual is a good day-by-day picture of his/her progress into or out of depression.

Looking back, my life seems like one long obstacle race, with me as its chief obstacle.

—JACK PAAR

Depression is a form of distress. While the same methods of treatment described in the last chapter can be used to alleviate it, depression has some unique characteristics that are worthy of special attention. We will look at depression in terms of (1) emotional disturbances, (2) physiological causes and (3) thought processes.

He won't get to the root of his problem, because the root of his problem is himself.

—CARROLL O'CONNOR
as Archie Bunker

EMOTIONAL DISTURBANCES

A variety of emotional events can be responsible for precipitating depression. About three-quarters of the population experiences mid-life depression. It starts when individuals begin to feel, as they enter mid-life, that the prospects for achieving their youthful aspirations are diminishing. It is common for these individuals to regret the way they have conducted their lives; their career choice; their choice of wife or husband; their financial status. They may feel entrapped and weighed down by their family and other responsibilities as they become aware that their desires for self-actualization and growth are yet to be, or cannot be, fulfilled. Their depression is based on guilt, self-recrimination and disappointment in themselves. Their feelings of anxiety are likely to be directed outside of themselves and to result in hostile feelings about others.

> *Depression is melancholy minus its charms.*
>
> —SUSAN SONTAG

Humor as treatment for the depressed individual helps relieve feelings of disappointment, guilt and lack of self-worth. There are two parts humor can play. If a person is only mildly depressed it is sometimes possible for him/her to respond to something completely madcap. Clowns, slapstick comedy or nonsense might direct the depressed person's attention briefly away from his/her self-derogatory feelings. Humor, particularly slapstick, has, on occasion, brought a seriously disturbed person out of a prolonged state of withdrawal or depression. Comedians, when they are particularly successful, say of their audience, "I killed them!" —when in reality they may have saved lives.

> *Humor is reason gone mad.*
>
> —GROUCHO MARX

The other way humor may help is when it causes the individual to view himself/herself objectively. This occurs when the humor is relevant to the individual's problems. How this happens is not well understood, but disturbed persons who have experienced it describe how their attention to the joke or other forms of humor caused them to get outside themselves for an instant. The problems did not change, but it seems that humor caused a part of their personality to split off and see their problems in a different light.

Kurt Vonnegut, in his book *Palm Sunday**, describes how his mother's suicide affected his life:

> The child of suicide will naturally think of death, the big one, as a logical solution to any problem, even one in simple algebra.
> QUESTION: If Farmer A can plant 300 potatoes an hour, and Farmer B can plant potatoes 50 percent faster, and Farmer C can plant potatoes one-third as fast as Farmer B, and 10,000 potatoes are to

---

*Excerpted from *Palm Sunday* by Kurt Vonnegut, Delacorte Press/Seymour Lawrence, New York, 1981.

be planted to an acre, how many nine-hour days will it take Farmers A, B and C, working simultaneously, to plant 25 acres? ANSWER: I think I'll blow my brains out.

Ken was a senior in a large high school that I visited regularly as a psychologist. He was referred to me because he had been sitting in class for a week in what was described as a dazed state. Although he was unresponsive and did no work, he continued to attend school. When I interviewed him, he spoke in a monotone and had the appearance of one moderately to severely depressed. He was preoccupied with thoughts of suicide and felt it was just a matter of time before he would end it all. His depression started when he had an accident while driving his best friend's car. His friend was injured, but not seriously. Ken blamed himself and expressed the wish that he had killed himself in the accident. He could see no purpose in continuing to live. School was a waste of time. Nothing gave him pleasure. He did not anticipate that things could or would ever be any better.

After I had tried every approach I thought might help him, Ken could still only see suicide as the solution. I then told him a few brief stories about persons who had attempted suicide and failed. I told a true story about a man who had prepared for his suicide in great detail. He locked the apartment door, placed a reading lamp in the oven and arranged chairs, a mattress and a pillow so that he could read while reclining in comfort with his head in the oven. He placed several of his favorite books within reach, turned on the gas and prepared himself for his comfortable exit from this life. All went well until the building manager smelled the escaping gas and broke in the door. The fire department revived him.

Humor is the sense of the absurd which is despair refusing to take itself seriously.
                                                    —ARLAND USSHER

Ken had paid attention and apparently had seen some irony in the story. He soon began talking about his feelings and frustrations. By the end of the interview he seemed much less intent on suicide, so I made an appointment to see him on the following day. At that time he was able to describe the change. The story about the man making elaborate plans to die had caused him to think about his own plans. He said that he looked at himself in the same way he had looked at the man in the story. He saw something ironic, but not something funny enough to laugh at, in his own situation. This started the process that resulted in his wanting to talk about his feelings and grapple with his problems. Ken is typical of many cases where relevant humor provided the turning point that helped a troubled person see his situation more objectively.

> *There seems to be no way to refute the logic of suicide but by the illogic of instinct.*
>
> —WILLIAM JAMES

It appears that a humorous statement introduced at the appropriate time in a therapeutic session is an ingredient needed to move the therapy into a positive channel. Dr. Alfred A. Bach provided me with the following examples from his own practice of psychotherapy. An intelligent young woman, with a good record of academic achievement, spent most of a therapy session expressing her low self-esteem. She dismissed Dr. Bach's reassurances and positive statements as insincere attempts designed to make a pitiful and unworthy person feel good. She said, "You talk like you think I'm stupid." He said, "I've been meaning to talk to you about that." This remark appeared ironic to her because she knew that she was not stupid. The comment indicating that stupidity might be her real problem caused her to counteract some of her own negative thinking, initiating realization of her own self-worth.

> *A person reveals his character by nothing so clearly as the joke he resents.*
>
> —G. C. LICHTENBERG

Whether or not humor can help individuals understand themselves depends on the degree of the humor's relevance, not the degree of fun generated. Comedy is an effective tool in getting an individual's attention away from a problem. Relevant wit helps the individual face his/her problem.

A depressed, guilt-ridden young man said to Dr. Bach, "I am

the kind of guy who just doesn't appreciate his parents. I must be worthless." Dr. Bach replied: "It is hard to appreciate parents who turn out such a worthless product."

When a self-pitying man said, "I feel anguish and indecision; if I give up being a nice guy I'll have to give up getting sympathy," Dr. Bach responded, "I can sympathize with you."

PHYSIOLOGICAL CAUSES

Severe and persistent depression is likely to have a biological basis. Research with antidepressant medicines has shown how body chemistry affects the ability of the brain and nervous system to respond. If the body is low in chemical neurotransmitters, the whole system becomes sluggish, resulting in depression. Hypoglycemia—low blood sugar— can make a person feel depressed as can many bodily illnesses. It is important, therefore, that the person suffering from a long-term, severe depression be diagnosed and receive medical or psychiatric treatment.

> *There are no such things as incurables; there are only things for which man has not yet found a cure.*
>
> **—BERNARD M. BARUCH**

Many persons become depressed during or following festive seasons. For example, some individuals have expectations that Christmas will be filled with joy, good will, and the warm family feelings they experienced when they were children. When they have expended great physical and psychic energy for Christmas and the magic doesn't happen, they blame themselves and go into a depression. It is also possible that biological causes are involved. Higher-than-usual intake of sweets causes a rapid increase in blood sugar, which results in an increased demand for insulin. The excess insulin then causes a condition of low blood sugar, which results in fatigue and depression. It is possible that if you overeat at mealtimes, nibble on sweets between meals and consume excessive amounts of alcohol for several days, any time of the year, you can suffer a mild depression afterward. It seems reasonable to assume that depression can be either biological, psychological, or a combination of both.

Although an adequate description of self-help methods for treatment of depression is beyond the scope of this chapter, Dr. Alfred A. Bach has provided a brief outline of some effective measures:

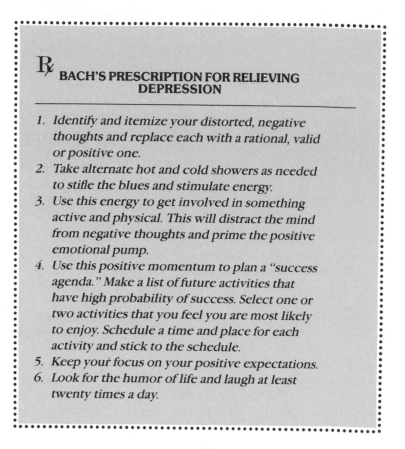

℞ **BACH'S PRESCRIPTION FOR RELIEVING DEPRESSION**

1. *Identify and itemize your distorted, negative thoughts and replace each with a rational, valid or positive one.*
2. *Take alternate hot and cold showers as needed to stifle the blues and stimulate energy.*
3. *Use this energy to get involved in something active and physical. This will distract the mind from negative thoughts and prime the positive emotional pump.*
4. *Use this positive momentum to plan a "success agenda." Make a list of future activities that have high probability of success. Select one or two activities that you feel you are most likely to enjoy. Schedule a time and place for each activity and stick to the schedule.*
5. *Keep your focus on your positive expectations.*
6. *Look for the humor of life and laugh at least twenty times a day.*

THOUGHT PROCESSES

In his book *Feeling Good: The New Mood Therapy*, Dr. David D. Burns describes his years of research on the causes and treatments of depression and presents a self-help treatment derived from that research. The method is a form of cognitive therapy that can correct our bad habits of thinking. Cognitive therapy helps the individual face the facts and correct the distortions that accompany depression.

Giving up self-deception is not an easy process, but the results are worth the effort. One may learn to conquer depression by changing the distorted patterns of perception that create and perpetuate negative moods.

> **Cognitive therapy is the first form of psychotherapy in history that has been shown in clinical research studies to be more effective than antidepressant drug therapy in the treatment of serious depression.**
> —DAVID D. BURNS, M.D.

Laughter's mental effect is to break away the dreads and fears that constitute the basis of so many depressions and lift one out the black hole of despondency.

Humor as therapy can effect many things:

• Humor has the power to reduce tensions and to create a relaxed atmosphere.

• It provides an outlet for otherwise unacceptable feelings, behaviors and impulses by facilitating talking about or acting out conflicts or emotions in a safe, nonthreatening way.

• Humor puts an individual in a frame of mind conducive to constructive interchange with others.

• Humor encourages communication on sensitive matters.

• Humor can lead to insight into causes of conflict and emotional disturbances.

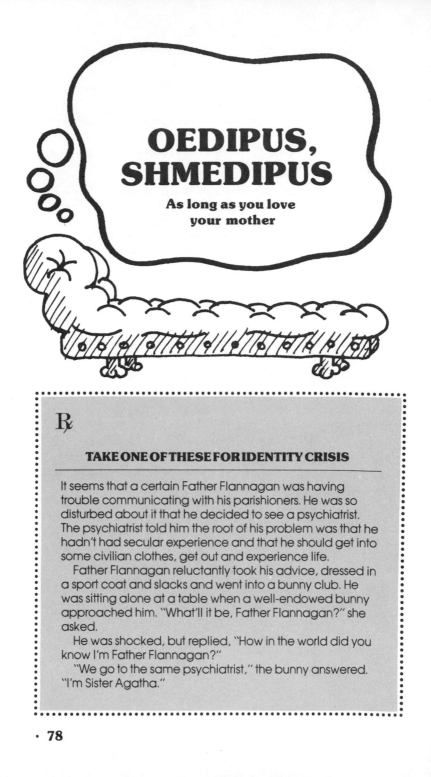

OEDIPUS, SHMEDIPUS

**As long as you love
your mother**

℞

TAKE ONE OF THESE FOR IDENTITY CRISIS

It seems that a certain Father Flannagan was having trouble communicating with his parishioners. He was so disturbed about it that he decided to see a psychiatrist. The psychiatrist told him the root of his problem was that he hadn't had secular experience and that he should get into some civilian clothes, get out and experience life.

Father Flannagan reluctantly took his advice, dressed in a sport coat and slacks and went into a bunny club. He was sitting alone at a table when a well-endowed bunny approached him. "What'll it be, Father Flannagan?" she asked.

He was shocked, but replied, "How in the world did you know I'm Father Flannagan?"

"We go to the same psychiatrist," the bunny answered. "I'm Sister Agatha."

PHOBIA UPDATE
BY BEATRICE SCHULAR[*]

Please add these new phobias to your phobia list:

CLAUSENPHOBIA,
Phear of Pickles

ANGORAPHOBIA,
Phear of Sweaters

PHOEBEPHOBIA,
Phear of Phoebe

*Ms. Schular has a fear of F's.

When a busload of people entered a large cafeteria, the group leader approached the manager.

"Sir, I'm Mr. Harris of the Halfway House. These nice folks are former mental patients. They've all been cured, but they do have one small idiosyncrasy: They'll want to pay you in bottle tops. Now, if you'll be so kind as to humor them in this way, I'll take care of the bill when they're through."

The manager, wanting to be a good citizen, went along and collected the bottle tops. The group's leader returned, and with gratitude said, "Thank you so much. I'll pay the bill now. Do you have change for a garbage can lid?"

● ● ●

"Our son thinks he's a chicken."
"Why don't you take him to a psychiatrist?"
"We would, but we need the eggs."

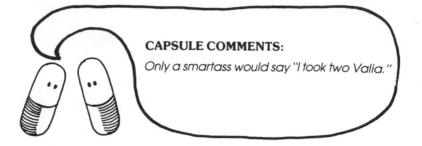

CAPSULE COMMENTS:

Only a smartass would say "I took two Valia."

"This psychiatrist told me if I had
sex with him once a day I'd be
much happier in my work."
"As a patient, you should report
this doctor."
"I'm not a patient, I'm his nurse."

YOUNG PSYCHIATRIST: "How do
you avoid getting depressed
listening to everybody's troubles
over all these years?"

OLD PSYCHIATRIST: "Who listens?"

OLDIES BUT OLDIES

People who find complete joy and fulfillment in the process of aging should be old enough to know better.

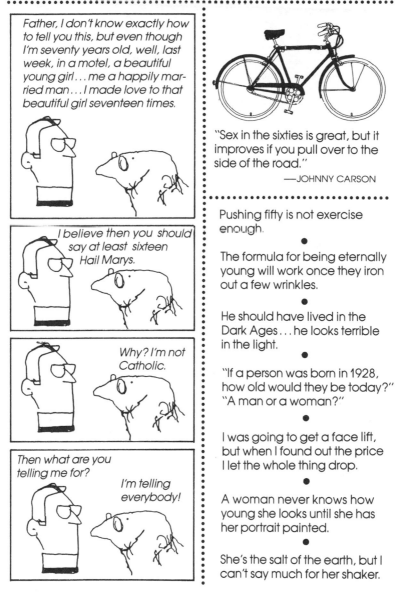

Father, I don't know exactly how to tell you this, but even though I'm seventy years old, well, last week, in a motel, a beautiful young girl...me a happily married man...I made love to that beautiful girl seventeen times.

I believe then you should say at least sixteen Hail Marys.

Why? I'm not Catholic.

Then what are you telling me for?

I'm telling everybody!

"Sex in the sixties is great, but it improves if you pull over to the side of the road."

—JOHNNY CARSON

Pushing fifty is not exercise enough.

•

The formula for being eternally young will work once they iron out a few wrinkles.

•

He should have lived in the Dark Ages...he looks terrible in the light.

•

"If a person was born in 1928, how old would they be today?" "A man or a woman?"

•

I was going to get a face lift, but when I found out the price I let the whole thing drop.

•

A woman never knows how young she looks until she has her portrait painted.

•

She's the salt of the earth, but I can't say much for her shaker.

LAWYER: *"I can't believe that at age eighty-seven, after sixty-eight years of marriage, you would want a divorce."*

OLD MAN: *"The marriage never worked. I never loved her... certainly didn't like her... I want out... just get me a divorce."*

LAWYER: *"But if you've been so miserable for all these years, why did you wait until now to try for a divorce?"*

OLD MAN: *"We made an agreement that we would stay together until the children died."*

BARUMP
BUMP

SINGER: "I'm always breaking into song."
CRITIC: "You wouldn't have to if you had the key."

●

DESK CLERK: "Did you find any towels in his suitcase?"
BELLBOY: "No, but I found a chambermaid in his grip."

●

"When it comes to spreading gossip, the female is much faster than the mail."

●

St. Peter asked a new arrival, "How did you get here so fast?"
The arrival replied, "Flu."

●

"Are you still engaged to the girl with the wooden leg?"
"No, we had a fight and broke it off."

HIGH & DRY

PERHAPS THE REASON WE JOKE ABOUT ALCOHOL IS THE
SAME REASON WE WHISTLE WHILE WALKING THROUGH A
CEMETERY AT NIGHT.

★ ★ ★ ★ ★

There are more old drunkards than old physicians.
—RABELAIS

Too much of anything is bad, but too much of good
whiskey is barely enough.
—MARK TWAIN

Once during prohibition, I was forced to live for days
on nothing but food and water.
—W.C. FIELDS

The worst thing about him is that when he's not drunk,
he's sober.
—YEATS

Drink always rubbed him the right way.
—OGDEN NASH

My grandfather would've discovered electricity but he was too poor to buy a kite. He had to hire one. Matter of fact, I have a picture of my grandfather standing in front of a saloon—hirin' a kite!

TEETOTALER: "If you pour water on a plant, it grows and thrives. Pour liquor on the same plant and it shrivels up and dies. Doesn't that teach you something?"
DRINKER: "Yes. If you want to grow a plant in your stomach, drink water."

•

The trouble with whiskey is that you take a drink and it makes a new man out of you, and then the new man has to have a drink.

•

Happiness is a large pitcher of martinis, a thick juicy steak and a big hungry dog to eat the steak so it doesn't go to waste.

•

They had a butler who drank too much...sort of an old family container.

•

A man called the stationmaster. "I left a bottle of white lightning on the train. I wonder if it turned up at the lost and found department?"
"No, but the fellow who found it did."

ABSTAIN FROM WINE, WOMEN AND SONG... MOSTLY SONG.

7.

Adjusting to Loss

●●

I can't live without that blanket.
I can't face life unarmed.

——LINUS

Some losses are inevitable. We will all lose our youth, eventually, unless we die young. We will all lose our lives at some time, and most of us will lose some of our loved ones. Even if we never get fired, we will still lose our jobs when retirement arrives. Apart from the inevitable losses common to us all, most of us will experience others. The breakup of a love affair can be traumatic, even when one recognizes that irreconcilable differences exist. The termination of a relationship, divorce or the loss of love is frequently followed by a period of depression. Separation from friends, or homesickness, produces severe anxiety and depression in some individuals. For some persons the aging process is cause for regret and sadness. Signs of age such as loss of virility, failure of memory, graying or loss of hair are grounds for panic.

Loss is a very subjective experience. The amount of grief depends upon the investment of self in the lost person, pet or possession. The greatest grief is usually over the death of a loved one, but some individuals experience great sorrow at the loss of money or a material object.

Experience is not what happens to you; it is what you do with what happens to you.

——ALDOUS HUXLEY

There is a major difference between the recovery from depression accompanying loss and recovery from the depression and anxiety described in the previous two chapters. When one experiences the deep emotional hurt brought on by loss, the depression results from grief rather than from self-hatred and guilt. It is essential that genuine grief be recognized and lived through rather than avoided or repressed.

The loss of a loved one through sudden death produces great shock and deep grief. The first response is shock and denial. "I know that death is real, but how can I let go of part of me?" "If my love is not dead, how can my lover be dead?"

With recognition that the loss is real, anger and depression emerge—anger at what has happened and depression over life without the loved one. Time brings understanding and acceptance, so that living becomes meaningful again.

Humor can play a valuable role in the process of accepting loss. An individual frightened by the emotional numbness or feelings of unreality brought on by the shock of death may find it helpful to share humorous recollections of the deceased. If the departed had talked about death, recollection of this can help the person in mourning accept its reality. Some famous persons of the past have left us amusing ideas about their own deaths. When Winston Churchill was asked if he feared death, he said, "I am ready to meet my Maker. Whether my Maker is prepared for the ordeal of meeting me is another matter." When Wilson Mizner was told that his death was only a few hours away, he rallied strength enough to send a postcard notifying a friend, "They're going to bury me at 9:00 A.M. Don't be a sucker and get up." About his funeral he said, "I want a priest, a rabbi and a Protestant clergyman. I want to hedge my bets." When Thoreau was asked, "Have you made your peace with God?" he replied, "We have never quarreled."

> *Excuse My Dust.*
> —DOROTHY PARKER [her own epitaph]

Do not deny the pain. If you are hurting, admit it. To feel the pain of desolation and the grief of loss is normal and proof that you are alive and able to respond to life's experiences. Don't try to run away from it or cover it up. The sorrow is washed away by weeping. Tears shed in response to grief must be accepted by friends and associates of the bereaved as an essential component of the recovery process. If attempts are made to hide sorrow from others, the grieving individual may hide emotions so well that he/she loses contact with the way he/she feels. In our society, we have long been taught to suppress tears. We should understand that weeping is not weakness but catharsis, and that failure to weep delays recovery and contributes to stress-related disorders.

Humor is an ally in helping us accept our own mortality and can be a comfort when we are bereaved.

> *Life does not cease to be funny when people die any more than it ceases to be serious when people laugh.*
> —GEORGE BERNARD SHAW

· ·

PETER-DANA ENTERPRISES, INC.

TO: ALL EMPLOYEES
FROM: BOARD OF DIRECTORS
SUBJECT: EXCESSIVE ABSENCE

Due to the excessive number of absences from the office, the following rules and procedures will be put into effect as of this date.

SICKNESS: Illness will no longer be an excuse. We will no longer accept your doctor's statement as proof, as we believe that if you are able to go to the doctor, you are able to come to work.

DEATH (other than your own): This is no excuse; there is nothing you can do for the deceased and we are sure that someone else with a lesser position can attend to the arrangements. However, if the funeral can be held in the late afternoon, we will be glad to let you off one hour early, provided that you plan your share of the work ahead enough to keep the job going in your absence.

LEAVE OF ABSENCE (for an operation): We are no longer allowing this practice. We wish to discourage any thoughts that you may need an operation as we believe, as long as you are an employee here, you will need all of whatever you have and you should not consider having anything removed. We hired you as is. To have anything removed would certainly make you less than we bargained for.

DEATH (your own): This will be accepted as an adequate excuse for your absence. We would appreciate two weeks' notice. We feel it is your duty to orient your replacement to your job.

ATTENTION: Entirely too much time is being spent in the restrooms. In the future, we will follow the practice of going in alphabetical order. For example, those whose names begin with "A" will go from 8:15 to 8:30. "B" will go from 8:30 to 8:45, and so on. If you are unable to go at your appointed time, wait until the next day when your turn comes again.

••

There are excellent books that can help you cope with the problems associated with death and loss. *How to Prepare for Death: A Practical Guide*, by Yaffa Draznieu, provides practical advice on all aspects of planning for your own death and for coping with the death of someone close to you. *Choose Life: A Philosophy for Today*, by Bernard Mandelbaum, is a collection of thoughts that can be of value for the individual confronted with loss. *Learning to Love Again*, by Mel Krantzler, is an excellent treatment of the problems of the recently divorced and is helpful to those who want to enliven or enrich their relationships.

We can prepare for some losses, such as retirement, or the losses associated with old age. We may look forward to taking it easy, and to the freedom from routine, without realizing how much work and those we associate with on the job mean to us.

> *Let me give a word of advice to you young fellows who have been looking forward to retirement. Have nothing to do with it. Listen: it's like this. Have you ever been out for a late autumn walk in the closing part of the afternoon, and suddenly looked up to realize the leaves have practically all gone? And the sun has set and the day gone before you knew it—and with that a cold wind blows across the landscape? That's retirement.*
>
> **—STEPHEN LEACOCK**

The nice thing about being retired is you have lots of time to read about what your problems are. There's more to retirement than reading the obituary columns to make sure your name is not in it. Retirement is a trap. As long as you stay in the rat race you're tense. Quit and you're past tense. But retirement doesn't have to mean you're a has-been. By making new friends and becoming involved in hobbies, community projects, a second career or other activities outside of your employment, before retirement, you can achieve a new and rewarding life-style and avoid the retirement blues.

> *When a man retires and time is no longer a matter of urgent importance, his colleagues generally present him with a watch.*
> —R.C. SHERRIFF

Don't be afraid to laugh at death, retirement, divorce or whatever your loss. Laughter is contagious. When you make others laugh, you help them and yourself. Look for humor in every event. Make a conscious effort to let laughter into your life. You can't force real laughter, but it must be allowed to happen. You have the best insurance available when you have learned to laugh—out loud—at life.

DIE LAUGHING

According to the *New York Times* of May 19, 1981, William Saroyan called the Associated Press five days before his death to leave a posthumous statement: "Everybody has got to die, but I have always believed an exception would be made in my case. Now what?"

Advertisement from Pittsburgh newspaper:

FOR SALE, SECOND-HAND TOMBSTONE. EXCELLENT BUY FOR SOMEONE NAMED MURPHY.

People are prohibited from picking flowers from any but their own graves.

It's hard to view one's own death objectively and still carry a tune.
—WOODY ALLEN

My uncle is a Southern planter. He runs a mortuary in Birmingham.
—FRED ALLEN

"How many of you would like to go to heaven?" the minister asked his congregation. All but one man raised their hands. "You mean to tell me that when you die, you don't want to go to heaven?"
"Oh, sure, but I thought you were getting a gang together right now."

● ● ●

UNDERTAKER: "Would you like your mother-in-law embalmed? Cremated? Buried?"
CHARLIE: "That'll be fine."

THE LAST WORD

John Barrymore:
SEE? I TOLD YOU I WAS SICK.

•

In Dodge City, Kansas:
HERE LAYS BUTCH,
WE PLANTED HIM RAW.
HE WAS QUICK ON THE TRIGGER
BUT SLOW ON THE DRAW.

•

JOHN GILLESPIE, 1882
HE DIED INSTANTLY WHEN HE WAS
SHOT IN THE HEAD, THE HEART AND
THE STOMACH.

•

In Tombstone, Arizona:
HERE LIES
LESTER MOORE
FOUR SLUGS
FROM A .44
NO LES
NO MORE.

•

In San Diego, California:
HE LIVED
HE DIED
HE CHOKED
HE CROAKED.

In Tombstone, Arizona:
CHAS. HELM, SHOT 1882
SHOT BY WM. McCAULSY. TWO HOT-
TEMPERED RANCHERS, WHO DIS-
AGREED OVER THE BEST WAY TO
DRIVE CATTLE.

•

A Madison, Wisconsin, lawyer:
THE DEFENSE RESTS

•

In Connecticut:
UNDER THIS SOD,
UNDER THESE TREES
LIES THE BODY OF JONATHAN PEASE.
HE IS NOT HERE
BUT ONLY HIS POD.
HE HAS SHELLED OUT HIS PEAS AND
GONE TO HIS GOD.

•

GEORGE JOHNSON
HANGED BY MISTAKE.

•

In New Orleans:
THIS IS WHAT I EXPECTED.
BUT NOT SO SOON.

INTER-OFFICE MEMO

TO: ALL STAFF
FROM: EMPLOYEE RELATIONS

IT HAS COME TO OUR ATTENTION THAT EMPLOYEES DYING ON THE
JOB ARE FAILING TO FALL DOWN. THIS PRACTICE *MUST STOP*, AS IT
BECOMES IMPOSSIBLE TO DISTINGUISH BETWEEN DEATH AND
THE NATURAL MOVEMENT OF THE STAFF.

PLEASE BE INFORMED THAT ANY EMPLOYEE FOUND DEAD IN
AN UPRIGHT POSITION WILL BE DROPPED FROM THE PAYROLL
IMMEDIATELY.

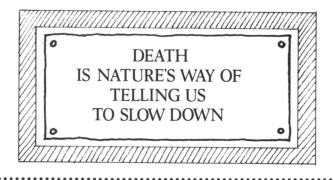

DEATH
IS NATURE'S WAY OF
TELLING US
TO SLOW DOWN

EUPHEMISM	REALITY
Aunt Emma passed away	Aunt Emma died
Uncle Harry went to the park	Uncle Harry died
The patient has expired	The patient died
My brother met his demise	My brother died
Grandpa has gone to his reward	Grandpa died
Grandma is with the angels	Grandma either died or was traded

"Kind of surprising to see an empty seat for this show, It's the hottest ticket in town."
"I can explain that. You see, my husband and I bought tickets for this show six months ago and since then he died."
"That's too bad. But couldn't you bring a friend?"
"No, they're all at the funeral."

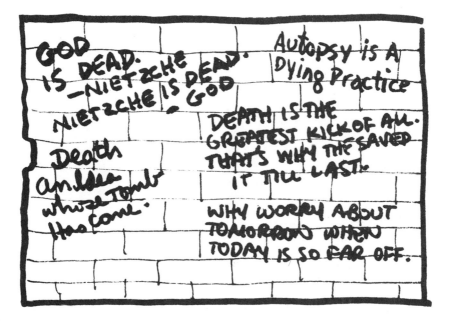

"Console yourself, madam. Heaven's mercies are infinite. There is another man somewhere, besides your husband, with whom you can be happy."
"There was. There was. This is his grave."

A HITHERTO UNPUBLISHED PRELUDE TO
FINNEGANS WAKE

Fade up on the interior of a bedroom in an Irish country cottage. The bed is occupied by Finnegan, a very sick man. His friend Pat stands beside the bed.

FINNEGAN

Oh, Pat . . . I'm goin' fast. Soon the Angel of Death will come and take me away to eternal damnation.

HARRIGAN

Shush, lad. You'll not be after talkin' like that. In no time you'll be swiggin' down a dram with all the boyos at Milligan's.

FINNEGAN

Do you really think so, Pat?

HARRIGAN

Think so . . . I know so! Just get yourself some rest and I'll tell Clancy and the boys you'll be joining us soon.

[*Pat turns to exit and inadvertently bumps his shoulder against the very narrow doorway.*]

HARRIGAN

They'll never get the casket through here.

Three people gathered at the casket of a friend. The first said, "In my culture it is said that if one places a little money in the casket, it will ease the departed's journey." He then placed ten dollars in the coffin. The second man did the same. The third man wrote a check for $30.00 and took the two tens.

• • •

The tombstone read:
HERE LIES
A LAWYER
AND AN
HONEST MAN.

A cemetery visitor remarked, "Times must be bad . . . they're putting them two to a grave."

In Las Vegas, a big-time gambler died. At the church, a friend gave the eulogy: "George isn't dead. He's only sleeping."

Called a voice from the back: "I've got a hundred bucks that says he doesn't make breakfast."

• • •

There was the Irish Catholic priest who said he'd rather die than be buried in a Protestant cemetery.

• • •

Mark Twain, about a politician: "I didn't attend his funeral, but I wrote a letter saying I approved of it."

HE: "Sweetheart, I hope you live forever plus three months."
SHE: "Why the three months?"
HE: "God forbid you should die suddenly!"

SQUAD LEADER: *Ready... aim...*
CONDEMNED MAN: *Down with Castro! Castro is a no-good rotten traitor!*
SQUAD LEADER: *Careful, amigo... that kind of talk can get you in trouble.*

BREAKING UP

DID YOU EVER CONSIDER DIVORCE?

DIVORCE?? ME? YOU JOKING? ME CONSIDER DIVORCE? MURDER, SURE BUT DIVORCE? NO.

There used to be a saying that a wedding is the only prerequisite for a divorce. There still is.

YOUNG ANON: We are allowed only one wife. This is called monotony.

"Pop, when did you learn to do frog impressions?"
"What are you talking about?"
"Well, mom said when you croak we'll all be rich."

That guy's had so many women his towels are marked "His" and "Next."

Talk to your plants. But don't expect much more help from them than you get from your psychiatrist.

THE HONEYMOON'S OVER
The room is dark. Man and wife are sleeping in twin beds. The husband stirs.

HUSBAND:
Honey...sweetheart...loverpie...

WIFE:
[*awakening*]
Yes, dear?

HUSBAND:
Why don't you come over and visit. I couldn't sleep thinking, "She's so near, yet so far."

WIFE:
Oh, how sweet.

[*The wife rises from the bed. Because of the darkness, she stubs her toe on an end table. The husband leaps out of bed reacting to her cry of pain and leads her to his bed. With soothing tones, he makes speedy love to her. The wife rises to return to her bed, again stubbing her toe.*]

HUSBAND:
Why don't you watch where you're walking, bumblefoot!

"What's the difference between
  stress and worry?"
"If your wife says she's pregnant—that's worry.
If your secretary says she's
  pregnant—that's stress."

IF IT'S YOUR FIRST TIME WITH YOURSELF... BE GENTLE.

Do you really love yourself or are you just fooling around?

FIND A RESTAURANT THAT SERVES CHATEAUBRIAND FOR ONE.

Be understanding and loving to yourself. But don't be a pushover.

WHEN YOU NEED HOLDING IS A GOOD TIME TO GET HOLD OF YOURSELF.

Treat yourself to something extravagant. It's affection buying but... so what.

WHEN YOU'RE ALONE IS A GOOD TIME TO GIVE YOURSELF A LITTLE PRIVACY.

"So, we were discussing with the marriage counselor whether Marge is dominating or not. First she told her side of the story. And then, she told my side of the story."

"Just this morning my husband said I was a terrible housekeeper. I got so angry I ran into the... uh... what do you call it?... oh, yeah, the kitchen."

LET'S CHECK IN TO
"CHEATING ARMS"

"It's only fair to warn you, my husband will be home in an hour."
"But I've done nothing I shouldn't have."
"I know, and if you're going to, you've got less than an hour!"

"My husband is the cheapest man in the whole world. I mean, he's cheap!"
[Husband enters]
"All right. This is it. You get behind her—I'm going to shoot you both."
"See, I told you he was cheap."

"Oh, my God, it's my husband!"
"Oh boy... I'm getting out of here."
"There's no way out."
"I'll jump out the window."
"But, we're on the thirteenth floor."
"This is no time to be superstitious."

[Husband bursts into bedroom surprising wife and lover.]
HUSBAND: What are you doing?
WIFE: [to lover]
I told you he was a dummy.

"I've always felt I don't want to die with my boots on."
"You may be in luck... here comes my husband."

"Hell hath no fury like the lawyer of a woman scorned."

INTERESTING REMNANT OF THE ME DECADE

Happiness depends on somebody else.
Where did that concept come from?
Mankind created it.
Is that the same mankind that created
    nuclear war and people who smoke
    cigars on elevators?
Yes.
Then maybe mankind goofed on this
    "lonely without somebody else" think-
    ing, too.

"What's the matter?"
"I just lost three wives in three months."

"What happened?"
"The first one died from eating poisoned mushrooms."
"What about the second one?"
"Same thing. Poisoned mushrooms."

"And the third one?"
"Fractured skull . . . she wouldn't eat the poisoned mushrooms."

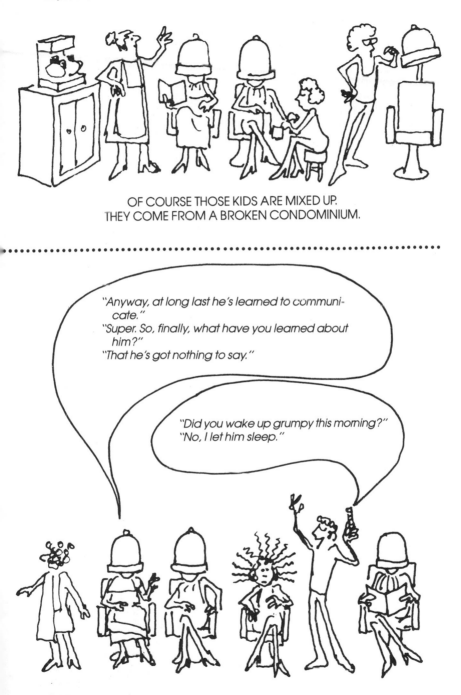

OF COURSE THOSE KIDS ARE MIXED UP.
THEY COME FROM A BROKEN CONDOMINIUM.

"Anyway, at long last he's learned to communicate."
"Super. So, finally, what have you learned about
him?"
"That he's got nothing to say."

"Did you wake up grumpy this morning?"
"No, I let him sleep."

"I'd climb the highest mountain, cross the burning desert, swim a raging river to be with my girl."

"When are you going to see her next?"

"Tonight . . . if it doesn't rain."

•

"I've seen you in the locker room wearin' a girdle. How long you been wearin' that?"

"Ever since my wife found it in the glove compartment."

•

"My wife's a light eater. When it gets light, she starts eating."

•

"Are birth control pills deductible?"

"Only if they don't work."

•

"I took my girlfriend out fishin'."

"Catch anything?"

"I hope not."

•

My old lady puts on those mud packs and all that grease. The other morning she chased after the garbage collector and said, "Am I late for the garbage?" He said, "No, jump in."

8.

Peter's Pharmacy

**Conquer Fear
and Frustration**

1. Learn how to cope with stress through study in the privacy of your own home.
2. Reduce anxiety with new self-help methods.
3. Overcome depression without spending time or money for psychiatrists.

BOOKS

How to Prepare for Death: A Practical Guide, Yaffa Draznieu. Hawthorn Books, New York, 1976.

Much of the trauma of death has a pragmatic base. The bereaved are at least as much in need of a good tax accountant, a forceful insurance agent or someone to do hardheaded bargaining with the mortician as of a clergyman or social worker. The author of this book gives explicit instructions for making decisions in all death-related circumstances—whether providing for your own or coping with either the expected or shockingly sudden death of someone close to you. Included are the various legal and practical problems survivors face.

Choose Life: A Philosophy for Today, Bernard Mandelbaum. Random House, Inc., New York, 1968.

The great thinkers of Jewish tradition, as well as the major secular figures of all civilization, provide thoughts of death, insight for the reader and a new realization of the value and joy to be found in "choosing life." The words of such men as Buber, Maimonides, Defoe, Camus, Gandhi, Thoreau, Molière and Adlai Stevenson are grouped in the concerns of each of our lives: community concerns, such as reducing ignorance, poverty and oppression; social concerns, such as learning the power of good action, providing for others, making a difference to our neighbors, friends, and family; and personal concerns, such as courage, creativity and excellence.

Learning to Love Again, Mel Krantzler. Thomas Y. Crowell Company, New York, 1977.

Written for people who are seeking a lasting love relationship and are finding it difficult to obtain, this book includes stories about real people, including the author and his wife. The four stages of learning to love again are covered: the Remembered-Pain Stage, the Questing-Experimental Stage, the Selective-Distancing Stage and the Creative-Commitment Stage. The author of the widely used *Creative Divorce* is writing for not only the recently divorced but the widowed, never married and happily married who wish to enliven and enrich their relationships.

Stress without Distress, Hans Selye, M.D. A Signet Book, published by New American Library, New York (originally published by J.B. Lippincott Company, New York), 1975.

The author presents his philosophy of life and guidelines to achievement, zest for life and free-

dom from the distress of unnecessary worry. Believing that man needs more natural ideals than those which presently guide him, Selye extrapolates from his understanding as an experimental biologist and expert on stress in describing his philosophy of "egotistical altruism." Utilizing stress in the right way, at the right level, for the proper length of time, we can add to the richness of our own lives and others.

The Relaxation Response, Herbert Benson, M.D. William Morrow and Company, Inc., New York, 1975.

Dr. Benson describes the history and development of, and research concerning, his own method for combating hypertension: a simply induced meditative state. The author tells in simple language how the reader can use the technique to reduce the stress of living in this age of anxiety. He shows how to achieve inner peace and calm in a few minutes a day, at home or at the office.

The Peter Prescription: How to Make Things Go Right, Laurence J. Peter. William Morrow and Company, Inc., New York, 1972.

This book puts forth a positive program for achieving happiness in our private lives and success and satisfaction in our careers. It presents twenty-five prescriptions for physical and mental health and happiness as well as instructions on how to achieve creativity, confidence and competence in your life style. Forty-four prescriptions for management competence are included. The book is written as satire, but carries a serious message.

Feeling Good: The New Mood Therapy. David D. Burns, M.D. William Morrow & Company, Inc., New York. 1980

The author presents a new approach—cognitive therapy—as a proven treatment for depression. The research was conducted at the University of Pennsylvania School of Medicine. Cognitive therapy is a major departure from Freudian analysis, behavior modification and psychopharmacology. It helps you take charge of your emotions, if you are willing to work at it. The book is written for both the lay person and the professional.

Dr. Bach's Prescription for Relieving Depression. Write: Alfred A. Bach, Ph.D., Malaga Cove Plaza, Palos Verdes Estates, California 90274.

AUDIO TAPES

The tapes presenting solutions for the problem of excessive anxiety or stress fall into two general categories: (1) those that use a problem-solving approach and (2) those that use induced relaxation, meditation or self-hypnosis. Those that involve the second approach should never be listened to when driving a car or when engaging in any activity that requires alertness.

Success without Stress, Bill Kenny. Write: Amacon, Dept. Q404, 135 West 50th Street, New York, New York 10020.

Bill Kenny's program will help the listener increase creativity, ease tension, improve concentration and indirectly contribute to health and happiness. It is a practical program designed especially for those who

work under stress. It has been presented at the Harvard Business School, at the MIT Sloan School of Management and at the John Hancock Life Insurance Company. Medical researchers have measured the *Success without Stress* program and found that it can result in lower blood pressure; improved respiration; a sharp decrease in infectious illnesses; improved sight, taste, and hearing; increased productivity and job satisfaction; reduced smoking; relief from insomnia; faster reaction time; improved attention; superior motor performance; better relations with workers. This program was produced by a division of the American Management Association.

Relaxation, Barry Konicov. Write: Potentials Unlimited, 9390 Whitneyville Road, Alto, Michigan 49508.

Barry Konicov, hypnotist, provides self-hypnosis instruction as a means of reducing anxiety. This is a useful technique for many in relieving uncomfortable and uptight feelings as well as helping to reduce high blood pressure, headaches and other health problems related to stress.

Effective Meditation. Write: Center for Bionostic Studies, P.O. Box 22946, Houston, Texas 77027.

This tape provides an explanation of five states of consciousness—concentration, meditation, contemplation, inspiration and illumination.

I'm O.K.—You're O.K., Dr. Thomas A. Harris. Write: Success Motivation Institute, P.O. Box 6714, Waco, Texas 76710.

Dr. Thomas A. Harris, psychiatrist, (he is author of the book by the same title) explains Transactional Analysis. The purpose of the present book is to help the listener gain insight and make behavior and personality changes so as to improve emotional adjustment and relationships with others.

How to Overcome Discouragement, Dr. Martin Kohe. Write: Success Motivation Institute, P.O. Box 6714, Waco, Texas 76710.

The author tells listeners how to overcome common problems facing the young, old, rich, poor and famous. The message is intended to provide assurance and inspiration so you can face the future with confidence.

Combating Depression: Self-help Techniques, Dr. Peter M. Lewinsohn. Write: BMA Audio Cassettes, 200 Park Avenue South, New York, New York 10003.

The listener learns to recognize cardinal signs of depression and understand its sources, especially those of social origin. Dr. Lewin-

sohn offers easily followed self-management strategies for dealing with environmental causes of depression and for developing skills to minimize their debilitating effects.

Psycho-Cybernetics, Maxwell Maltz, M.D. Write: Success Motivation Institute, P.O. Box 7614, Waco, Texas 76710.

Maxwell Maltz, M. D., the author, explains how to apply the power of self-image psychology toward achieving a more fulfilling life. Many have found his technique to be helpful in combating mild depression and in making their lives more of what they wanted them to be.

Death, Grief and Bereavement, Dr. Elisabeth Kübler-Ross, Dr. Jeannette Tolta, Dr. Robert Fulton, Dr. George G. Williams, and others. Write: Charles Press Publishers, Bowie, Maryland 20715.

This is an extensive series of cassettes that includes lectures, interviews, dialogues and discussions on matters related to death.

PART III

Communicating Successfully

●●●

How to Talk Funny

9.

Witty Conversation

●●

> *Conversation laid the foundation*
> *of the civilization we are dedicated*
> *to defend.... Great books, scientific*
> *discoveries, works of art, great*
> *perceptions of truth and beauty in*
> *any form all require great conversation*
> *to complete their meaning.*
> —A. WHITNEY GRISWALD

A young man was invited to a party so that he could meet some important people. Naturally, he was on his best behavior. As he was entering the room where the guests had gathered, he caught his toe on the edge of the rug. Although he made frantic efforts to regain his balance, he landed sprawled on the floor in front of everyone. As he picked himself up he said, "I also do card tricks." This little joke gained him the admiration of all present and turned what could have been an embarrassing or awkward social situation into a personal victory.

A witty conversation is an exchange of spontaneous remarks in which each contribution builds upon the last. It cannot be repeated or reproduced. Even when recorded, it loses its impact on second hearing. Most wit is germane only to the context of a particular conversation.

> *The hero of the small-town theatrical performance was to jump into a river. As he leaped offstage, the sound-effects girl was supposed to make the appropriate splashing sounds in a tub of water.*
>
> *One night, however, she missed her cue, and the actor hit the floor with a mighty thud, but no splash. There was a moment of dead silence. Then, out of the wings, came the feeble voice of the actor: "My goodness! The river is completely frozen over!"*
>
> —GENE BROWN

Conversation can be the serious discussion of a most-important issue or the social chatter at a cocktail party. Whatever the level of the conversation, wit or humor can provide the social lubricant that keeps the exchange moving. The most effective way of establishing communication with a stranger, or re-establishing communication with an acquaintance, is to break the ice with a humorous remark.

As a tool of human interaction, wit can make others feel either accepted and understood, or ridiculed and rejected. It can sharpen the cutting edge of a verbal stab at an opponent, or offer the protective cushion of compassion to one who needs it.

> *The real wit tells jokes to make others feel superior, while the half-wit tells them to make others feel small.*
>
> —ELMER WHEELER

Wit that helps us laugh "with" others is a potent force for solving problems. When we laugh "at" other persons or groups, we are excluding them from our sympathy, appreciation and understanding. When we laugh "with" them, we are embracing them with our empathy and love. Sharing humor creates a bond between people. It says "We both see, understand and enjoy." The shared memories of the funny stories of old friends cement relationships. Wit offered to a stranger is usually accepted as an offer of good will.

One holiday evening, a kindly and witty man, Mac Mason, was at the checkout counter of a supermarket. People in the long lines were impatient and irritable and the clerk looked weary and harrassed. As she began to ring up his order, Mac leaned forward and said, "Gift-wrapped if you don't mind." As her initial horror dissolved into a smile, she relaxed, and the smile of gratitude remained as evidence that she knew a sympathetic customer was laughing with her about the situation and not at her for her fatigue.

It is a great misfortune neither to have enough wit to talk well nor enough judgment to be silent.

—JEAN DE LA BRUYÈRE

Adding a ridiculous element, such as exaggeration, is often a way to express empathy with another. Scotty Wuerker received a phone call from a dear friend, Mary, who asked her to dinner. Scotty felt somewhat embarrassed because she had accepted three of Mary's dinner invitations, and had not had the opportunity to offer an invitation in return. Scotty feebly protested, "But I already owe you forty-seven dinners!" Mary said, "It's really fifty-nine, but who's counting?" This humorous response was interpreted by Scotty as laughing with her over the feeling of awkwardness of the situation, so she accepted happily. Mary's quick quip was superior to a serious discussion about the unimportance of "keeping even" among good friends.

Betty Ann Daley contributed a story about a young lawyer, Eugene Kennedy, newly hired by the Bank of America. He was told to go to the home of a wealthy dowager to discuss the administration of her estate. The butler ushered him into a large, dimly lit room where the lady was seated in the far corner. As he drew near, she said, "Good evening, young man. Tell me all you know. It won't take long." The moment he saw the twinkle in her eye marked the beginning of a long friendship. In the following years, during which he administered her estate, she never failed to greet him with "Good evening, young man. Tell me all you know. It won't take long," and he never failed to appreciate the way in which she had put an unsure, young lawyer at ease. Without the kindly attitude, the greeting could have been devastating. With it, he realized that she understood how he felt and could laugh at the situation with him.

It's not so much what you say as it is the person you are while you're saying it.

—BAYARD RUSTIN

The common element in these stories is that the humor was directed at the situation. This allowed the participants to come together and laugh at the situation and share the joke. There is a fine line between "laughing at" and "laughing with" another person. It is the attitude of the person presenting the witty remark that makes the difference. This attitude, or the feelings behind the words, is called the metamessage. Humor is frequently communicated as much—or more—by the metamessage as by the words. When an old friend greeted me with "Peter, you old bastard, what kind of mischief have you been up to?" the words were insulting, but the message I received had nothing to do with my parents' marital status or my assumed indiscretions. The metamessage says, "Peter, I'm glad to see you—tell me what you've been doing."

In *Meta-Talk and How to Read a Person Like a Book*, Gerard I. Nierenberg and Henry Calero discuss how the words we say are completely overwhelmed by the feelings expressed in our physical attitudes and movements. The authors encourage us to become more aware of those feelings and to incorporate them more honestly into what we say in order to produce a greater integrity in our communication. They suggest that the more you use talk that is flavored with the appropriate attitudes, the more people you will have to talk to and the more people will talk to you.

> *For good or ill, your conversation is your advertisement. Every time you open your mouth you let men look into your mind.*
>
> **—BRUCE BARTON**

A charming conversationalist is one who reminds others of things to say and then listens while they say them. Joke telling is not conversation. It can add to the pleasure of any conversation, but it cannot compare with the pure delight of an appropriate exchange of spontaneous wit. True wit causes the mental juices to flow and the levels of mutual appreciation to rise.

In many social situations, we sit for long periods, so that respiration becomes shallow and circulation becomes sluggish. The physical activity of laughter contributes to conversation because it increases circulation and respiration and brings about a feeling of euphoria or well-being. This restores our zest for mental activity and social interaction.

Humor is an attitude, a way of looking at life that takes in all sides of things—the serious, the ironic, the absurd and the funny. It opens new dimensions in conversation by seeing beyond the obvious or trite. In *How to Talk with Practically Anybody about Practically Anything*, Barbara Walters suggests that a sincere compliment is a good conversation opener—with anyone. You are not offering just a platitude; rather, the approach requires you to focus on the good qualities of the person to whom you are speaking—a great attitude with which to begin any conversation.

In almost every social situation, sharing laughter solidifies the group and stimulates interaction. When members of the group are unburdened of anxiety, stress and conflict, their outlook is brightened. Laughter is socially contagious. In any group, if one or two start laughing, soon others will follow. Contagious waves of laughter appear to be automatic responses of the diaphragm and respiratory organs. Attempts to stop this response often cause the laughter to become more explosive.

Men and women have an equal capacity for laughter, so we can assume that they have equal aptitudes for humor. An obvious difference between male and female humor is that males are more frequently the narrator of jokes in mixed-sex social situations. This is probably a result of traditional sex-role expectations in our society. It is an act of social assertiveness to assume the role of joke teller or storyteller, and it is a violation of cultural expectations for the female to aggressively dominate mixed-sex social interaction.

> **Whether women are better than men I cannot say—but I can say they are certainly no worse.**
>
> **—GOLDA MEIR**

Apparently, in all male or all female groups the telling of stories and jokes occurs with almost equal frequency. This indicates that a joke-telling ability and sense of humor are human characteristics possessed by both sexes. As women become increasingly liberated from the traditional, socially imposed female roles, we should see more female joke tellers. Recent years have borne witness to an increase in the number of professional women comedy writers and performers. May this encourage women everywhere to speak up and share their sense of humor with us all.

A WITTY CONVERSATIONALIST BECOMES A PROFESSIONAL PERFORMER

One of the best of the new breed of female comics is Geri Jewell, a young, pretty, brilliant and very funny comedienne whose most distinguishing characteristic as an entertainer is her cerebral palsy. The symptoms of her disorder—the uncontrollable jerky movements, the speech problem and an uneven gait—cannot be hidden. Geri has learned to use her problem as the basis of much of her humor, both on stage and in conversation. Once when she arrived at a restaurant for a luncheon meeting with me, the parking attendant assumed that she was drunk and said, "Lady, you've had enough." He was extra careful in making certain that she put her parking ticket in her pocket for safekeeping. She said to me, "I won't need the ticket. He won't forget me, and he'll remember my handicapped car, the one with the door that sticks in the wide-open position." When our waiter brought our lunch, she held up her hands, displaying their organically driven movements, and said, "I used to be a waitress...they didn't like the way I tossed salads, so I went to work at Shakeys. I want to get a job at Sloppy Sam's...the food's so bad that it should be thrown around." Throughout our lunch, she responded with humor to every situation that could be an embarrassment if taken seriously.

As a child, Geri attended special schools for the physically handicapped in Orange County, California. She became a regular student at Fullerton Junior College, where she majored in psychology. She then studied theater arts at Cypress College, where during her freshman year she became acutely aware of the sympathy and guilt that her condition aroused in others. After a struggle with herself that lasted several months, she decided to devote her life to comedy and to never, ever, use guilt exploitation in coping with her handicap. She was fortunate in that her drama professor accepted her unconditionally and encouraged her in her ambition.

Geri Jewell, at twenty-four years of age, has mastered the use of humor in conversation and in coping with the problems of living with her handicap. She has taken this same humor to nightclubs, the stage and television and is building a successful career as a performer.

Today, as a comic, Geri makes her uneven way on stage, reaches the microphone, stands in the spotlight, looks around, makes eye contact with her somewhat uptight, embarrassed audience, and says, "I have a secret I am going to confess to you. I have cerebral palsy." With her first laugh, the anxiety begins to vanish and a friendly relationship develops. As she continues, the laughter mounts, and the handicap is no longer a barrier to communication. "One day I went out and bought a T-shirt. It said, 'I don't have cerebral palsy. I'm drunk.' They charged me thirty-five cents a letter for this thing. I wished I had polio—it would have been a lot cheaper.

"When I go into a liquor store to buy a bottle they think I'm already drunk. Sometimes I can't get over all the money you people spend just to walk the way I do. I'm one of the few people who drive better than I walk. I've been pulled over only once for my driving, but I've been stopped four times for my walking."*

R̶

CONVERSATIONAL PRESCRIPTIONS

1. *Inject a few raisins of conversation into the tasteless dough of existence.*
   —*O. Henry*
2. *One of the best rules in conversation is: never say a thing which any of the company can reasonably wish had been left unsaid.*
   —*Jonathan Swift*
3. *Never speak unless you can improve the silence.*
   —*Vermont proverb*

*Permission to print granted by the author.

COMMUNICATION

The nuclear missiles which may someday fall on Washington and Moscow will probably be just dropped communications.

COCKTAIL PARTY *CON*-VERSATION

"Yes, I'm of the Jewish persuasion, but you can find schmucks in any religion."

•

"I visited the home of Evelyn Waugh and her sister was there too."

"She accused me of thinking of nothing but sex. Boy, I sure could use a piece of beer."

•

"England is fine as long as you remember that they're on the decimal system, ten pounds to the dollar."

"Talk about heritage, my family and myself have lived in Frisco for generations."

•

"Oh, yes, man, all us jazz musicians are hep to that bebop."

MIGUEL MOUSE
A LESSON IN COMMUNICATION

There was un ratoncito, a little mouse, and he was hiding in his little hole in the living room. He was very frustrated, because he knew where there was some queso, some cheese. But, he heard the "miao" of el gato, the cat.

This was no ratoncito estupido, because he knew that gatos eat ratoncitos. So he waited until he heard "Woof, woof," and he knew it was el perro, the dog. He knew that perros scare away los gatos, and also that perros don't eat ratoncitos. So he walked out and saw, no perro, pero el gato!

And el gato gulped him up and said: "Que bueno ser bilingue!" "How great to be bi-lingual!"

"What did you do in England?"
"Punting, on the Thames."
"Oh, I've been there. Passed through on my way to Stratford-on-Avon. It was good to see where those door-to-door products come from."

"I've been with the Met for twenty-five years. I was on the same bill with Pavarossi and Boris Goodenov."
•
"Oh, to be in Munich, or Munchkin as we say during the Septemberfest."
•
"Richard Burton axed me to be his dialogue coach."

"Myself and any other chemist can tell you there's nothing better for the bod than good old H_2A."

The act of mounting a horse—
GEDDINON
The act of dismounting a horse
—**GEDDINOFF**
> UNDERACHIEVER COWBOY: *[to his horse who got its hoof caught in its own stirrup]* Ay, if you're **GEDDINON**, I'm **GEDDINOFF**.

IBIN SEEN—to have had in one's vision
JUSS—only
> UNDERACHIEVER: **IBIN SEEN** spots before my eyes.
> ACHIEVER: Did you see a doctor?
> UNDERACHIEVER: No, **JUSS** spots.

Fowl cooked in deep fat—
FRYCHICKIN
To be consumed—**EDEN**
By themselves—**SEPPUTLY**
> UNDERACHIEVER ONE: Should **FRYCHICKIN** be **EDEN** with the fingers?
> UNDERACHIEVER TWO: No. The fingers should be **EDEN** **SEPPUTLY**.

Travelling through the air—**FLINE**
> UNDERACHIEVER: When I sleep on my belly I dream I'm **FLINE**.
> ACHIEVER: Why don't you sleep on your back?

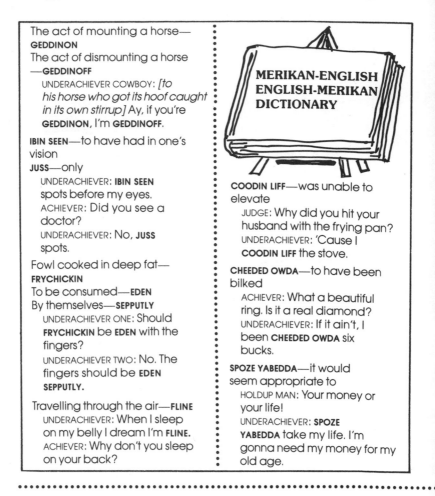

MERIKAN-ENGLISH ENGLISH-MERIKAN DICTIONARY

COODIN LIFF—was unable to elevate
> JUDGE: Why did you hit your husband with the frying pan?
> UNDERACHIEVER: 'Cause I **COODIN LIFF** the stove.

CHEEDED OWDA—to have been bilked
> ACHIEVER: What a beautiful ring. Is it a real diamond?
> UNDERACHIEVER: If it ain't, I been **CHEEDED OWDA** six bucks.

SPOZE YABEDDA—it would seem appropriate to
> HOLDUP MAN: Your money or your life!
> UNDERACHIEVER: **SPOZE YABEDDA** take my life. I'm gonna need my money for my old age.

IF I WANT YOUR OPINION, I'LL GIVE IT TO YOU.

**COWBOY/ENGLISH
ENGLISH/COWBOY
DICTIONARY***

FADE—to serve food
HINS—female fowl
BOWLED IGGS—breakfast
favorite
It was so hot we had to **FADE**
ice cream to the **HINS** to keep
'em from laying **BOWLED IGGS**.

HEP—assistance
He's as much **HEP** as a one-
legged man in an ass kickin'
contest.

HAIR—to perceive sound
I'd lay forty miles of communication line under combat conditions to **HAIR** her burp on the
phone.

HAIL—the back of the human foot.
He's so dumb, he couldn't pour
beer out of a boot if the directions was wrote on the **HAIL**.

Without funds—**PORE**
We're so **PORE** if a thief breaks
in all's he'll get is practice.

A declaration of independence—
ARMAGEDDON
When they **DRAP** the bomb
ARMAGEDDON outa here.

To let fall—**DRAP**

City in state of Washington—
SADDLE
I hear tell they got a might
healthy climate in the Northwest.
Why in **SADDLE** they had to
shoot a man just to start a
cemetery.

a blink of the eye—**WANK**
state of slumber—**SLAPEIN**
Were you **SLAPEIN** with my
wife???
Not a **WANK**.

MEMO

TO: JESSE JAMES
        DODGE CITY

FROM: WELLS FARGO

Dear Sir:

Enclosed please find the schedules and route changes you
requested. Hope you find your
travels with us rewarding.

---

*excerpt from The Cowboy/ English- English/Cowboy Dictionary, BB, N.Y.

A rustic man stands beside a
rather ferocious-looking hound.

STRANGER: Your dog bite?

RUSTIC: Nope.
[*The dog suddenly bites the
stranger.*]

STRANGER: I thought you said
your dog didn't bite!

RUSTIC: That ain't my dog.

A beautiful zebra making her
first visit to a farm had asked
what all the animals did. The
cow said she made milk. The
chickens said they laid eggs.
The sheep said he made wool.
The stallion said, "Take off those
crazy pajamas and I'll show
you."

If you have to go to the bathroom, raise your eyebrow

During the war, FDR ordered a blackout in some Washington buildings. The message came back for his approval: "Illumination must be extinguished when premises are not in use." Roosevelt lost his temper and bellowed: "Dammit—why can't they say 'Put the lights out when you leave.'"

•••

Dear Dad,
You haven't sent me a check in two weeks. What sort of kindness is that?
                    Your Son
Dear Son,
That is known as unremitting kindness.
                    Your Father

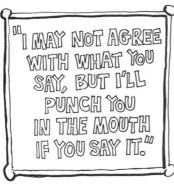

"I MAY NOT AGREE WITH WHAT YOU SAY, BUT I'LL PUNCH YOU IN THE MOUTH IF YOU SAY IT."

•••

With most people who say "That goes without saying," it doesn't.

"George, do you think Ronald will ever speak?"
"I don't know. The doctors say if he hasn't spoken a word in fourteen years, chances are he never will."

"This is awful!"
"Ronald, why haven't you said anything before???"

"Up till now, everything's been okay."

MAN: Hello, may I talk to Harry, please?

MALE VOICE: There's no Harry here

MAN: Is this 987-6655?

MALE VOICE: Yes.

MAN: Are you sure?

MALE VOICE: Did I ever lie to you before?

• • •

GIRL: Hello.

WOMAN'S VOICE: Sweetheart, I heard you weren't feeling too well. Look, darling, I'm going to bring over your favorite chicken soup, and for dessert your favorite chocolate mousse. Don't you worry, Susie, your mother will come over and cheer you up.

GIRL: I'm sorry, but there's no Susie at this number.

WOMAN'S VOICE: Oh, excuse me . . . I must have misdialed.

GIRL: Gee . . . does that mean you're not coming over?

"My policy is to say nothing too sharp about my political opponents, and nothing at the expense of world peace, and certainly nothing in bad taste . . . so, goodnight."

10.

Effective Speaking

●●●

Spartans, stoics, heroes,
saints and gods use a short
and positive speech.

—RALPH WALDO EMERSON

It is not the purpose of this brief chapter to explain the art of
public speaking, but only to show how to use humor to make
speaking more effective communication. The following comments are not intended to apply to stand-up routines or humorous
lectures presented for entertainment purposes only.

> *My father gave me these hints on speech-making: Be*
> *sincere . . . be brief . . . be seated.*
>
> —JAMES ROOSEVELT

A speech is a sequence of four parts: (1) the introduction, (2)
the opening, (3) the body and (4) the closure.

THE INTRODUCTION

If you are asked to introduce a speaker, find three or four
accomplishments that represent the speaker's qualifications. The
addition of a humorous anecdote that epitomizes the speaker's
humorous or good qualities provides the ideal ending for the
introduction. I have never heard of a speaker, or even an audience, complain about an introduction being too short.

Remember that an introduction is a prologue, not a catalogue. The introduction should set the scene for the speaker. When you are the speaker, you know the kind of receptive mood you want from the audience. If the introducer creates a wrong audience expectation, you will be off to a poor start and will have to use the opening of your speech to correct the false expectation. Beatrice Lillie, the internationally famous comedienne and star of British reviews, was married to Sir Robert Peel. Bea Lillie had a reputation as one of the funniest women in the world. Once when she was introduced by an overzealous chairman as Lady Peel, she was greeted with polite applause and had great difficulty getting laughs. The audience's attitude was one of respect. It was not considered polite to laugh at the antics of a member of the nobility.

If you want your audience to respond to your humor, you will get off to a good start with an introduction that presents you as a humorous person. If you want serious attention paid to your research or accomplishments, the introduction should focus on your solid accomplishments. You must decide how you want to be presented—as the expert authority, problem solver, planner, inspirer, discoverer or wit. You should provide the chairman with appropriate information and with a request for a brief introduction.

The best guarantee of an introduction that will be a prologue to your speech is to write it yourself. This will be greatly appreciated by your introducer. It will make him/her look good. It is a favor to your audience, because it will save them time and give them exactly the information they need to appreciate your speech to the fullest.

> *A good talker or writer is only a pitcher. Unless his*
> *audience catches him with heart and mind, he's*
> *defeated.*
>
> **—WILSON MIZNER**

For example, I wear two hats. Most of my professional life has been spent in teaching and in doing research on teacher effectiveness. I have published a series of textbooks on teacher competence and have received a number of awards for my research. My sideline is writing satire. I have made thousands of appearances as a satirist on radio, television and the lecture platform If an introducer presents a list of my academic achievements, professorships, scientific publications and awards, the audience rightfully expects to hear a serious message about education, not a humorous lecture about *The Peter Principle*. Therefore, it is important for me to have a different introduction for each topic. When I am to give a humorous lecture, I provide the following type of introduction, which may be changed if the emcee wishes.

Introduction

Dr. Peter, who is not as tall as Wilt Chamberlain but considerably taller than Woody Allen, was born and semieducated in British Columbia, Canada, and now lives it up in southern California.

Dr. Peter is best known for his satirical writing. *The Peter Principle* was an international bestseller for more than a year. It has been translated into thirty-seven languages and has sold millions of copies. His other successful books are *The Peter Prescription, The Peter Plan, Peter's Quotations* and *Peter's People*.

Dr. Peter feels that, as an outsider, he can be completely objective about the human race. He claims that success has not changed him and that he is still the same confused, egotistical person he was before he became so famous.

Each of his books came into being when he couldn't find a book on a subject he wanted to know about—so he solved the problem by writing one. There is so much Dr. Peter doesn't understand that he will never run out of material to write about. Already some of his writing is so profound that it is beyond his own comprehension. Some of his books are funny and some are serious—he is not sure which is which.

Your speaker—Dr. Laurence Peter.

THE OPENING

The purpose of the opening of a speech is to win the audience's favorable attention to you and, in particular, to your subject matter. The former is achieved by your platform manner, your self-confidence and desire to communicate, your knowledge of your subject and your preparation, experience and practice as a speaker. The latter is where humor can be your ally or enemy.

We all know that it is common practice to open a speech with a joke or funny story. This is said to be desirable, because it is an attention grabber that gets the speech off to a good start. However, research shows that this is only partially true.

The joke can be your enemy as well as your friend if it does not pertain to your subject matter. If it is simply an extraneous "I'm reminded of a funny story," you can experience a condition in which the funnier the joke the more interference with your theme. Seek out the blockbuster, but let it somehow be germane to the issue and thereby enhance communication.

R̥

PRESCRIPTIONS FOR THE INCLUSION OF HUMOR IN YOUR SPEECH OPENING

1. *Use humor that is relevant to your topic.*
2. *Provide a transition from your joke or story to your topic.*
3. *If you don't have relevant humor, just introduce your topic by asking your audience a provocative question about your subject, and then launch directly into the body of your speech.*

Here is an example of humor in the opening of a speech that is an integral part of the content. When I spoke on the subject of "How Rational Are We?" I opened with the question, "Is there a truly rational person among us?" I then proceeded to tell the true story of a reporter's visit to the office of the great Danish physicist, Niels Bohr—the scientist who detailed the structure and function of atoms and laid the foundation for quantum mechanics. As the reporter entered Bohr's office, he noticed a horseshoe hanging on the wall. He asked Bohr if he believed the horseshoe would bring him good luck. The great scientist replied, "I believe in no such thing. Not at all. I'm scarcely likely to believe in such foolish nonsense. However, I am told that a horseshoe will bring you good luck whether you believe in it or not." Because the audience responded favorably, it was not difficult to then direct their attention to the influences of mind and emotion.

You may write your own jokes or adapt existing material. If you were called upon to speak about cutting back on credit in order to slow inflation, you might write an opening, such as: "I'm getting mad! For years my bank has been forcing credit cards on me. Now, overnight, they are trying to make me feel guilty for using them. It's like taking me to a pastry shop and then telling me to go on a diet. My wife's credit card was stolen. I did the patriotic thing. I didn't report it. The person who stole it spends a lot less than my wife."

Next, inform your audience what you are going to tell them by (1) defining the subject of your talk and (2) briefly specifying what you are going to say about it. Now move quickly into the body of your speech.

The finest eloquence is that which gets things done.
—DAVID LLOYD GEORGE

THE BODY

Your opening has won favorable attention, and it is now essential that the body of your speech achieve momentum immediately and maintain it all the way to the climax. In planning the body of your lecture, spend all the time required to assure that the climax is well thought out. What is your objective? How can it be stated most effectively? Do you want your audience to be persuaded to believe in something—conservatism, liberalism, socialism, Buddhism, unidentified flying objects, conservation? Do you want people to know something—the hazards of smoking, how to manage household finances, how to tame a wild coyote? Do you want action—votes for yourself or another candidate, donations for a charity, people to lose weight and live longer, pledges of support for a conservation project? Whatever your purpose, it must be clearly defined and attractively presented.

If you don't know where you are going, you may end up someplace else.
—LAURENCE J. PETER

To get from the opening to your objective, arrange your facts, arguments and illustrations in a series of steps leading up to the climax. In delivering these steps stress the key words. Change your vocal pitch—lower your voice in presenting the important phrases. Vary your rate—move rapidly over unimportant words and slow down for the important ones. Pause before and after important ideas.

In using humor to emphasize the points along the way to your objective, the same principle of relevance applies. The reason for inclusion of each humorous item is to move the audience in the same direction as the serious message of the speech.

Occasionally a humorous story, or a joke consisting of a scene, a situation and a punchline, can be effective, but usually brief humor in the form of quotes, aphorisms, laws, quips and one-liners is more effective in keeping the speech moving forward and is much easier to present. The point is made quickly. The humor is not aimed at getting the big laugh and thus does not interrupt the momentum. Brevity is still the soul of wit.

When President Coolidge was asked what a preacher had said in a sermon about sin, he replied, "He was against it." When President Truman was interviewed about his "Give 'em hell, Harry" reputation, he said, "I never give them hell. I just tell them the truth, and they think it's hell." Whistler, the great American painter, said, "If other people are going to talk, conversation is simply impossible." These statements may not be great laugh-getters, but they do have elements of humor and could be used to make points about brevity, truth and the art of conversation. In selecting quotes, choose ones that are direct and that do not contain difficult or foreign words: their effect in a speech must be immediate.

> *The Romans would never have found time to conquer the world if they had been obliged to learn Latin first.*
> —HEINRICH HEINE

When discussing corruption you could quote George Bernard Shaw: "A government that robs Peter to pay Paul can always depend upon the support of Paul," or Goodman Ace: "I keep reading between the lies," or Tom Lehrer: "Life is like a sewer—you get out of it what you put into it." When dealing with military fiascos or man's inhumanity to man, one is reminded of Groucho Marx's:

"Military intelligence is a contradiction in terms," or Leonardo Da Vinci: "Truly man is king of beasts for his brutality exceeds theirs," or Will Rogers: "You can't say civilization don't advance. In every war they kill you in a new way," or Pogo: "We has met the enemy, and it is us." When describing our confusing times what could be better than Irene Peter's: "Today if you are not confused you are just not thinking clearly," or Woody Allen: "I'm afraid of the dark and suspicious of the light," or Morrie Brickman: "I don't know whether the world is full of smart men bluffing or imbeciles who mean it," or Clarence Darrow: "When I was a boy, I was told anybody could become President; I'm beginning to believe it," or H. Mumford Jones: "Ours is the age which is proud of machines that think and suspicious of men who try."

Anonymous one-liners can do the same thing.

Jumping to conclusions seldom leads to happy landings.

A weakness of this age is our inability to distinguish our needs from our greeds.

The hardest thing to learn is which bridge to cross and which to burn.

The girl that is easy to get may be hard to take.

Xerox is a copying device that can make rapid reproduction of human error, perfectly.

You'll find in no park or city, a monument to a committee.

The cost of living is going up and the chance of living is going down.

Write your own funny lines, adapt and personalize one-line jokes from other sources or select what you need from books or articles.

During the primaries a baby in New Hampshire had been kissed by so many candidates, she had chapped cheeks. Every time she hears "My fellow Americans," she puckers up.

The most depressed man I ever met had been arrested for indecent exposure—and then released for insufficient evidence.

Do you know why the experts at this convention keep referring to conventional wisdom? I've been to a lot of conventions and I've seen very little.

We have advice to give and warnings to make. The problem is our warnings are like that of foghorns—they call attention to the fog without doing anything to lift it.

In my opinion, which I seldom respect . . .

This is one of the few places where you can enjoy yourself—without having a good time.

Thanks for making me honorary chairman. It's like being the man who turns the pages for a pianist—he has to be there, but who else cares.

It's great to share this podium with another Canadian. Someone who hasn't been a credit to his country, either.

My hometown in Canada was just a narrow place in the road. The good thing was there was no crime in the streets. We had crime but no streets.

I would swallow my pride but I hate junk food.

How can I soar like an eagle when I'm working for these turkeys?

I hate taking naps. Waking up once a day is bad enough.

My mother and father fought constantly. If it wasn't me arguing with him, it was me bickering with her.

I hate being misquoted because I can't stand to have other people's feet in my mouth.

Two types of speakers I'd like to eliminate—those who never stop to think and those who never think to stop.

When you have made your points and enhanced them with humor, and have reached your objective, it is time for the closure.

THE CLOSURE

You have achieved your objective, and even if you haven't it is too late to do anything about it. Anything more that you try to say will be counterproductive. All you have to do now is stop talking as gracefully as possible and sit down. Appeal for action by saying that the solution is in their hands. It is up to them to vote, contribute, support, believe, feel, understand or do whatever your speech was intended to accomplish. Then finish with a statement that will leave them laughing or smiling, such as: "I don't want to close—you have been so kind." Or, make a light-hearted remark, such as: "As you leave this hall tonight, I'd like you to remember one thing—where you parked your car"; "I leave you with the words of Luther Burbank, 'Never look down on a lily—tomorrow it may be looking down on you' "; "Before I go, I leave you with this thought: Keep your words soft and sweet—you never know when you might have to eat them some day"; "Be good to each other and may you live among people who care"; "Let me leave you with the words of Elbert Hubbard: 'Don't take life too seriously; you will never get out of it alive.' "

℞

PRESCRIPTIONS FOR EFFECTIVE USE OF HUMOR IN PUBLIC SPEAKING

1. *Be introduced by a brief statement that is a prologue to your speech. Provide notes that include only what you want said, or write the introduction yourself.*
2. *Open by obtaining favorable attention to yourself and your topic. Tell a humorous anecdote, story or joke that is relevant to your subject— or don't tell a joke at all.*
3. *Develop your message through humor that is an integral part of that message.*
4. *Summarize your points and make your conclusion or climax clear and sincere.*
5. *Close quickly with humor that will leave your audience with a good feeling.*

POINT MAKERS

As a tool for communication, the joke is peerless. The executive in the office motivation mode, the speaker who must do the same in public or anyone who must drive home a point cannot find a more practical support system than a repertoire of jokes, one-liners, anecdotes, bits and pieces designed for allegorical use.

Most joke books categorize items by general headings, such as profession, nationality or area of interest. Few have attempted to gather jokes designed for the transference of emotional impact. Here follow examples of humor which illustrate Fear, Pride, Devotion to Duty, Happiness, Love ... all the big-name emotions.

PREJUDICE

The minister of food distribution announces that those forming a line in Red Square at six o'clock in the morning will receive food, vodka and chocolate. An endless line forms in front of the Kremlin. At seven o'clock an announcement is made that since there was not sufficient food for everybody so would all Jews kindly leave the square. These announcements continued deleting categories of people until at three o'clock the next morning, without one slice of bread being distributed, there were only a handful of old Reds left. They too are told to go home empty-handed. As they are wearily leaving Red Square one of the old-timers turns to his comrade and says, "Sure, the Jews only had to wait one hour!"

YOU'RE NEVER TOO OLD

INSURANCE MAN: Now to complete this application ... How old was your father when he died?

CLIENT: Did I say my father is dead? He's healthy as an ox.

INSURANCE MAN: Then, how old was your grandfather when he died?

CLIENT: Did I say my grandfather died? He's the rogue of Sun City and a scratch golfer.

INSURANCE MAN: Oh. Well, how old was your great-grandfather when *he* died?

CLIENT: Did I say my great-grandfather died? He's 126 years old and just got married.

INSURANCE MAN: Why would a 126-year-old man get married?

CLIENT: Did I say he *wanted* to get married?

QUICK THINKING

A man approaches a clerk in a supermarket.

MAN: I'd like to buy a half of a head of lettuce.

CLERK: I'm sorry, we don't sell half heads.

MAN: Why should I pay for something I'm going to throw away? [*He leaves*]

MANAGER: What's up?

CLERK: Some dummy wanted to buy a half a head of lettuce [*notices the customer has heard his put-down and continues without missing a beat.*], and this kind gentleman has consented to buy the other half.

•

MANAGER: Son, you've done so well, I'm going to make you manager of our Toronto branch.

CLERK: If you don't mind, sir, I'd rather not. To me all Canadians are either hookers or hockey players.

MANAGER: My wife happens to be Canadian!

CLERK: Really? What team does she play for?

NOT-SO-QUICK THINKING

JUDGE: You're accused of driving while drunk.

DRUNK: Not me, your honor...as soon as I realized I was bombed, I moved over to the passenger's side.

UNFORESEEN EVENTS

Often, if one compares the gravity of one's own problems with those of others, it can help soften the blow.

If you think you've got trouble...

The scene: The Vatican. A wild-eyed cardinal enters. He approaches the Pope in a state of near hysteria.

CARDINAL: Your Holiness...on the phone—it's...it's...it's...Jesus!

POPE: Why are you so alarmed? We knew this would happen some day.

CARDINAL: But he's calling from Salt Lake City!

COPING WITH GOVERNMENT

You can't fool all the people all the time. That's why we need a two-party system to get the job done.
—MARK TWAIN

DEVOTION TO DUTY

A commando leader addressing his men: "Men, tomorrow's raid will be the toughest and bloodiest we've ever tackled. The enemy already knows we're coming and they're reinforced by tanks and paratroopers. It'll be 200 of them to each of us. The planes may not have enough fuel to get back if there are any survivors. Now, we leave at 0700 hours sharp. Anybody who's late doesn't get to go."

FEAR

A married woman and lover in bed. A noise is heard.

WOMAN: My God...that's my husband!

MAN: Where's your back door???

WOMAN: We don't have a back door!

MAN: Where would you like one???

● ● ●

"I opened the closet door and there was a skeleton!"

"Did you run?"

"I don't know...but I passed some folks who were running."

DRINKING

You're not drunk if you can lie on the floor without holding on.
—DEAN MARTIN

FUN

Most of the time I don't have much fun. The rest of the time I don't have any fun at all.
—WOODY ALLEN

THE WORK ETHIC

A tester in a brewery had worked there for thirty years and had, in the process, become a hopeless alcoholic. One day he stumbled on a catwalk over a huge vat of beer and drowned. The superintendent, whose sad chore it was to tell the man's widow of the tragedy, revealed the details of the mishap. The wife said, "Well, at least I have the consolation that beer was Harry's life and that he died happy." The superintendent replied, "Died happy...he got out three times to pee!!"

CONFIDENCE OR OVER-CONFIDENCE

A bounty of $1,000 per captured Arab had turned Ari and Uri into fortune hunters. Day and night they scoured the desert looking for their valuable prey. Exhausted, they fell asleep dreaming of their potential fortune. Suddenly, Ari awoke to see that they were surrounded by 100 Arabs with bayonets and automatic weapons pointed down at them. Ari nudged Uri and said, "Uri, wake up. We're rich!"

CONVERSATION CONDIMENTS

To relieve the symptoms caused by feeling less sophisticated and "with-it" than your fellow man or woman, try sprinkling these various words and phrases randomly throughout appropriate conversations. Use these spicy entries as your starter kit.

Don't worry about knowing the meanings of the words and phrases. That is a redundant function.*

CAPITALIST	JOCK	INTELLECTUAL
supply-side	flea flicker	de rigeur
hardball	momentum	plethora
nukes	living legend	Nouvelle Vague
big board	hat trick	'ludes
time share	Heisman candidate	read-out
OPEC	go for broke	Weltanschauung
trending	paid attendance	momento de verdad
spokesperson	sudden death	cinéma vérité
rhetoric	nose guard	bio-feedback
input	mathematical	DNA
pragmatic	probability	Native American
tax shelter	stats	nouveau
capital gain	money player	ciao
across the board	naked reverse	Pritikin
revenue enhancement	bonus baby	freeze frame
gobbledygook	fly pattern	je ne sais quoi
target marketplace	free agentry	the cube
damage control	era	territorial imperative
premature obituary	rbi	zap
disincentive	designated lover	preppy
bracket creep	the scent of blood	Chuck and Di
economic malaise	fancy schtick	penetration
validity of the basic	the backhand blues	mojo
optimal	clothesline tackle	truncated
cost-effective	dunk dunces	underwhelmed

*Redundant function is good anywhere.

CAPITALIST	JOCK	INTELLECTUAL
viable	double dribble dilemma	panache
Camp David	turnover trauma	paladin
stagflation	whiff	clone
crisis-prone	taxi squad	underlying motivation
dissident	rude dude	swingles
political posture	bowl fever	procreation
grievous misconception		SoHo
narrowcasting		quixotic
empirical underpinning		herpes
mandate		propensitease
context		franchement
double-digit		
low profile		
stock and bondage		
survival economics		
Rage-onomics		
go for broker		
trending		

11.

Problem Solving

●●

*There comes a time in the
affairs of men when you
must take the bull by the tail
and face the situation.*
—W.C. FIELDS

When you arrive at the edge of a cliff and are facing an abyss, it is best to stop and look around rather than to keep moving forward. When confronted by an obstacle, or a problem, we should face it objectively and try to see its importance and its potential danger to our well-being. Humor can help us see the problem in perspective. It cannot, in and of itself, solve most problems; we need to use all of our relevant knowledge, common sense, professional skill and technology to resolve our personal, business, industrial and social problems. In applying our rational powers, humor often can be the catalyst that makes the process work. In problem solving, humor isn't trivial. It should be used to deflate the overinflated, not to trivialize that which is genuinely important.

*My way of joking is to tell the truth. It's the funniest
joke in the world.*
—GEORGE BERNARD SHAW

Laughter at new ideas can retard progress. New ideas, innovations, designs, discoveries and inventions can be frightening and, frequently, can threaten the status quo. There is a tendency to ridicule that which is novel in order to preserve our security or complacency.

Humor can inhibit the problem-solving process when it deflects our focus away from the causes of difficulties. When channeled, it penetrates our traditional defenses and throws new light on life's absurdities.

> *What I want to do is to make people laugh so that they'll see things seriously.*
> —WILLIAM K. ZINSSER

In the following examples, we see some ways in which problem solving through humor can be effective.

A FEW QUIPS IMPROVE MOOD

My daughter Alice was aboard a plane that had been delayed for over an hour in takeoff. The passengers had been in and out of their seats and many were grumbling. When the time arrived for the passengers to return to their seats, the pilot said, "Ladies and gentlemen, will you please clear the aisles and sit down so I can see out of the rearview mirror and back this plane out." As the plane taxied out to the runway, he made a few more humorous remarks. At takeoff, the passengers were relaxed and in a better mood.

During a discussion or argument there are times when just the appropriate and relevant quote, law, joke or quip is the ingredient needed to move the discussion in the direction of a resolution. A good example occurred during a heated debate on economy when Arizona congressman Morris Udall suggested that the Post Office be put in charge of the inflation problems: "They wouldn't solve it, but they'd certainly slow it down."

INCOMPETENTS GET THE BIRD

> *Wit sometimes enables us to act rudely with impunity.*
> —DUC DE LA ROCHEFOUCAULD

James H. Boren, president of the International Association of Professional Bureaucrats, has a unique way of using humor to get results. He has created a zany-looking sculpture of a featherless bird that is presented to incompetent bureaucrats, along with the association's diploma certifying them as members of The Order of the Bird. What is unique is not the humorous idea of awarding a ridiculous and embarrassing prize that draws attention to the recipient's incompetence, but the method of its presentation.

In 1969, Albert Pacheco worked at the U.S. Naval Shipyard in Yokohama, Japan. While undergoing spinal surgery at the Naval Hospital, the surgeon's scalpel slipped and injured the spinal cord. Mr. Pacheco lost the use of his legs. His claim for compensation benefits was passed back and forth between Navy and Labor bureaucrats for nine years. Dr. Boren and his association determined that bureaucrats that could keep a claim alive for nine years without paying one penny in benefits to Mr. Pacheco deserved some public recognition.

> *Guidelines for Bureaucrats: (1) When in charge, ponder.*
> *(2) When in trouble, delegate. (3) When in doubt,*
> *mumble.*
>
> **—JAMES H. BOREN**

The International Association of Professional Bureaucrats determined that the responsibility for action in Mr. Pacheco's case was that of the Department of Labor. A formal letter of nomination for the Order of the Bird Award was sent by Dr. Boren to the Department of Labor. The department was informed that it would be only a matter of time before the twenty-nine coordinating committees gave final approval for the award to be official. The Department of Labor was assured that the presentation ceremony would be an impressive affair that would receive full news coverage.

Bureaucrats do not appreciate having their nonresponsiveness exposed to the public eye. At least, in this case, Assistant Secretary Daniel Elisburg wrote to James Boren within ten days to inform him that the Office of Workers' Compensation Programs had approved Albert Pacheco's claim. Boren's procedure of informing the Department of Labor of the nomination, but referring the final approval to multiple coordinating committees and delaying all public announcements until the award received official approval, was a stroke of bureaucratic brilliance. It gave the Department of Labor plenty of lead time in case they wished to take corrective action, while avoiding the appearance of a threat of exposure. Who could misconstrue bureaucrats—"referring to committees," "obtaining official approval" or "impressive ceremony with full news coverage"—as an example of putting on the heat?

Bill Forington, an inventor in Denver, developed a new rotor system for a helicopter, but couldn't get approval from the Federal Aeronautics Administration (FAA) for a trial flight. Eventually, he tethered his craft and hovered six inches off the ground. The FAA launched legal action to collect a $2,000 fine for his lack of a pilot's license and air-worthiness certificate. Actually, the FAA had no jurisdiction as long as the craft was tethered, so Boren's association nominated the FAA for the Order of the Bird Award. The FAA dropped the charges against Forington before the committee had time to finalize the award, so once again the Bird was not presented. Boren had used bureaucratic delay as a way to smarten up a bureaucracy.

> *The nearest thing to immortality in the world is a government bureau.*
> —**GENERAL HUGH S. JOHNSON**

When nomination for an Order of the Bird Award does not produce immediate results, Boren persists. When Hertz received a nomination for the practice of confirming auto reservations without checking to see if cars were available—which resulted in reservations and no cars—the company ignored the impending award. It also declined to attend the Awards Banquet, so the Bird was presented in absentia. The company officials must have been displeased with the news coverage and Boren's subsequent discussions of the matter on television's "Today Show" and Tom Snyder's former "Tomorrow Show."

At the next Awards Banquet, Hertz sent a company representative to accept the Bird and to tell Boren, "We decided you were not going away, and we want to get the Bird out of circulation." Later, the representative assured Boren that they had tightened their practices and were making computer checks now before confirmations.

BETTER MOTTOES

I am privileged to be a member of, and at times president of The Let's Have Better Mottoes Association, Inc.* This organization is the brainchild of its sponsor and secretary, John Yeck of Dayton, Ohio—a pioneer in the direct-mail marketing business. Mr. Yeck, while providing his client companies with direct-mail letters and advertising, conceived the idea of providing them with some humor each month in the form of a motto and a monthly report of the activities of the association. A few of the unique characteristics of the association are: (1) There is no way for you to join. You simply are notified that you have been nominated for membership. (2) You are sent a Resignation Blank in case at any time you wish your name to be stricken from the membership list. It is suggested that you should do this if you believe the association to be too highbrow. (3) Resigned members are furnished with a De-Membership Card stating that they are not now, and never have been, a member. (4) A member whose motto is chosen is nominated to be president for a month. (5) Unlike the moralistic, inspiring mottoes of yesteryear, those of The Let's Have Better Mottoes Association, Inc. are uninspiring, antiuplifting and certainly not complimentary.

A man who can smile when things go wrong has found someone to blame it on.

I hate intolerant people.

Nepotism's not bad if you keep it in the family.

Logic is the art of going wrong with confidence.

He who hesitates gets bumped from the rear.

To err is human...to forgive is against company policy.

Never lend money to a friend. It ruins their memories.

Beware of those who say they're on your side...so's appendicitis.

Knowledge is power...if you know it about the right person.

The Association is John Yeck's vehicle for using humor to create good will in the business firms that are his customers or

*"Better Mottoes" Association, Inc.; P.O. Box 225; Dayton, Ohio 45401

best prospects. Helpful though these gags and funny lines are, many problems require a more logical, rational or scientific approach that demands a sustained effort.

HUMOR AT THE CONFERENCE TABLE

Meetings, committees, task forces, commissions and other team efforts organized to make plans and solve problems should begin with clear objectives. This involves defining, delineating and exploring the problem.

A film manufacturer called a meeting of department heads to try to find the cause of the failure of their bulk cut film. The product, perfect upon leaving the factory, deteriorated rapidly. The problem was presented and each department representative contributed his explanation.

The chemical research department claimed the film was completely stable under all normal storage conditions. The chemist felt that the new opening on the film boxes was defective. The packaging department representative shot that argument down by showing that the deterioration of the film was uniform throughout the package. The packager was emphatic that the quality control department was negligent. Quality control was convinced that the problem was in the retailer's handling of the film. He felt that it was the sales department's responsibility to check the storage conditions at retail outlets. The sales manager assured those attending the meeting that his people were well aware of the expiration dates and retail environmental conditions. He stated that the defect was in the chemical content of the film. The head of chemical research defended his earlier statement by presenting evidence proving the superiority and stability of the emulsion. He also indicated that the sales manager might not be able to understand the scientific evidence, but that he could assure everyone present that his statistics were conclusive.

Obviously, the meeting accomplished nothing. Later, it was revealed that a chemical defect in the paper used to separate the sheets of film had caused the deterioration. Apparently the supplier of the separating tissue had made a minor change in its manufacturing process that left a chemical trace, causing the film emulsion to deteriorate. Each individual believed that he was presenting facts, but as it turned out, none of their conclusions were correct. Each member was committed to defense of himself/herself and his/her own department.

How could humor have contributed to an earlier solution? Had the meeting opened with some good-natured kidding and joking about the problem and had the chairperson been the target of some of his opening remarks, the committee members could have been less defensive. This is no guarantee that every time you tell a story you solve a problem, but humor could have created an environment in which the participants felt less defensive and more like members of a team.

An opening remark, such as, "You all know what the problem is. Our bulk film, in spite of all of our best efforts, has a serious flaw. It fails to meet our expectations, and does not live up to its guarantee. We are all uncomfortable to be in the position of the fly-by-night manufacturer that guaranteed his product would last right up until you need a new one. At this time, we don't have a clue as to the cause of the problem. It may not be our fault. If we blame ourselves, it might be like blaming beds for causing the sexual revolution. My ignorance cramps my style, so I turn the discussion over to you to explore all the possible sources of this problem."

> **Everybody is ignorant, only on different subjects.**
> **—WILL ROGERS**

Humor makes the participants feel that they are not going to be put on the spot. By humorously suggesting that the cause might lie outside the present committee, the members could have broadened their vistas and explored more possibilities. Through the chairperson's remarks that made fun of his own ignorance, he set the scene for others to help him. Paraphrasing and personalizing well-known quips creates good feelings in others and enhances their effectiveness. The chairperson could have said, "Five years ago when I took this job as assistant general manager I thought I understood all the problems in the business. This situation proves me wrong, but it's too late. I can't quit now because I like the job too much. I'm a modest man. I have much to be modest about. There's an old saying, 'Nobody is perfect,' and I am a perfect example of that saying."

Be humble or you'll stumble.

—DWIGHT L. MOODY

When you make yourself the target of your own quips, others will like and admire you. When others like you they are inclined to like what you represent. This builds trust that helps others to become involved and use their own potential more fully.

My greatest strength as a consultant is to be ignorant and ask a few questions.

—PETER DRUCKER

Humor that is relevant and encourages the participants to focus on the task at hand is the most effective. It is more important for the group leader to bring the problem down to a human scale with mild humor than it is just to get laughs. It is better to convey the message that you are able to think funny than it is to convince them that you are funny.

The one thing all charming people have in common, no matter how they may differ in other respects, is an amused detachment from their commonplace troubles.

—SYDNEY J. HARRIS

Rational thought about solving problems requires that the problem first be clearly defined, that the criteria for a solution be established and that all possible solutions be considered to see if they meet the criteria. In the case under discussion the difficulty should have been defined as a problem that (1) started on or about a specific date, (2) affected the total area of the sheets of film and (3) occurred progressively and uniformly over time under a variety of storage conditions. Every possible cause should have been considered, including everything with which the film came in contact. Humor could have been used to facilitate each phase of this rational process.

Although the humor to solve the case was discussed in terms of the leader of the group, it could have been used in similar ways by any or all of the individuals that comprised the group.

Imagination is more important than knowledge

—ALBERT EINSTEIN

R̥

PETER'S PROBLEM-SOLVING HUMOR PRESCRIPTIONS

1. THINK FUNNY. *Humor is easier to recognize than to analyze or understand. Try to see the problem from a different or unusual point of view. If your view or idea amuses you, try it out on others. Judge your humor by their response.*
2. ADAPT MATERIAL. *Use humor from any source. Personalize it and change it to suit your situation or the problem at hand.*
3. BE THE TARGET. *Tell stories, jokes, anecdotes, quips and one-liners about yourself. Nobody will resent your laughing at yourself. When you treat yourself lightly and poke fun at your weaknesses, looks or mistakes, you show others that you are open, vulnerable and trusting. This encourages others to be free and risk a little, with the result that lines of communication are opened. Furthermore, if you laugh at yourself first, your kidding and joking about others is more acceptable. This will also make your own burdens lighter.*
4. SHARE YOUR HUMOR. *By sharing your sense of humor and by doing and saying funny things, you will not only provide laughter and happiness but will help others to a new perspective of their problems. You can take almost any disagreement, any wrong or injustice, any gripe or any difficulty and use humor to change things for the better.*

HUMOR MAKES THE POINT

William McAllister, a quality control engineer for a major airline, described a meeting that consisted of a hot debate on the wisdom of refitting some aging aircraft with modern jet engines. The protagonists pointed out the fuel saving, the quietness and the improved reliability of the new modern engines. The antagonists pointed out the current age of the air frames and the other components. The chairman broke the smoldering impasse and restored the group's good humor when he said, "Some of us are concerned about these geriatric old ladies we have come to like. Others amongst us liken this operation to a bosom transplant for their grandmothers. Maybe wasteful, maybe not...but grandma might be delighted."

Probably, the participants' laughter was in response to the similarity of the visual image of the old plane with a pair of new jet engines and an old woman with a pair of new breasts. I cannot say whether the prospect of improving Grandma's sex life influenced their decision, but for whatever reason, the new engines were approved.

William McAllister provided another example of humor as a problem-solving technique. Each year, the chief statistician of the airline's technical department was required to make a presentation to the flight crews showing the performance standards of the aircraft in the fleet.

The statistician was worried because the pilots never paid much attention to his statistical displays. Further, he suspected that they did not understand what the curves on the charts meant and seemed confused as to whether an ascending curve was good or bad. His illustrator hit upon the novel idea of placing small thunder clouds on the poor performance side and shining sunbursts on the good performance side.

The pilots were amused, paid much better attention and seemed to derive more meaning from the statistics thereafter.

SICK AND HEALTHY HUMOR

There is general agreement that humor is healthy when it relieves tension and restores perspective. It is not always possible to respond immediately with humor. We are progressively con-

fronted with the deeply tragic aspects of our existence, making
objectivity more and more difficult. At what point is humor that
makes light of tragic situations counterproductive? If the humor
reduces or removes our resolve to do something constructive
about a pathological or evil condition, it is truly sick humor. On
the other hand, much that is called "sick humor" is only different
or new humor that dares to treat subjects—such as death, violence and hostile feelings—that society traditionally has repressed
or regarded as being incompatible with humor.

> *A man walking at night sees a light in the window and
> says, "A mother praying for the safe return of her boy."
> A second man sees the light and says, "Oh boy, hanky-
> panky going on up there!" The second man is a censor.*
> —GOODMAN ACE

Just this side of the thin line that separates healthy from sick
humor is the insult joke that accurately reflects an individual's
problem so that he/she gains insight. When I was a school
psychologist, a teacher, Miss Boyle, visited me regularly to complain at length about the density and stupidity of her pupils. On
one visit we had exchanged a few humorous remarks, including
a story of a boy handing his father a report card full of failing
grades and saying, "I don't know whether it's caused by heredity
or environment." The time seemed right so I told Miss Boyle
about a teacher who said to her class, "I've explained this three
times and it's perfectly clear to me." Miss Boyle laughed and our
discussion indicated that she had seen herself in that story.

Although humor that reflects an individual's problem is sometimes effective, it is quite risky. I taught with Harry, who had a
compulsion about being on time. He bragged about his punctual-
ity and was critical of anyone who failed to meet his standards of
split-second timing at period changes and other daily schedules.
In the staff lounge, I told a story about a young fellow who was
so punctual that management decided to promote him into a
supervisory position. He is still punctual and now makes all his
mistakes right on time. Harry was incensed. He was not only
angry with me, but subsequently became more critical of those
he perceived as careless about the matter. His haranguing was
counterproductive in persuading others to be more punctual
because they were not motivated to emulate him. He had a

well-deserved reputation for being lazy as well as for the poor
quality of his teaching. A psychological explanation of his hostile
response to my attempt at humor would be that I had attacked
the area of his perceived competence. My lack of sensitivity in
this situation was evident, but there is no way to be always
right when humor reflects on another's behavior. Probably the
best way to handle the situation you create when a joke backfires
is to explain that you were only joking and to apologize for the
hurt that it caused.

> *There are two insults which no human will endure:*
> *the assertion that he hasn't a sense of humor, and the*
> *doubly impertinent assertion that he has never known*
> *trouble.*
> —SINCLAIR LEWIS

A joke may be effective in making a humorous comment about
an individual's behavior and appear to have a desirable result,
but still produce an unexpected negative outcome. As a committee member I attended a series of planning meetings for the
development of a school psychology program. One member,
Carl, was extremely negative. He knew that whatever was pro-
posed wouldn't work. His wet blanket approach had effectively
dampened the spirits of those with sparks of ideas to contribute.
Ideas were not flowing. Carl's favorite and oft-repeated comment
was, "That's easier said than done." He had repeated his favorite
squelch several times when I said, "That's easier said than done—
unless you are a stutterer." The group seemed amused and Carl
reduced his number of negative remarks. I was pleased with this
response. After the meeting a member came to me and suggested
that I should be ashamed of myself for making fun of stutterers. I
explained that I had not intended any ridicule of stutterers and
that there were none at the meeting. He replied, "My best friend
is a stutterer and I found your remark offensive." Although I
believe this kind of response to be rare, there is always the
possibility that a person will respond negatively to an innocent
remark. This is unavoidable, so we should always be prepared for
the possibility that our humor will not be perceived as amusing.
Individual perception, by its nature, is unique. We can never be
in exactly the same place as another person at exactly the same
time, so even if we were all alike, our perceptions would not be
identical. We should try to understand the other person's view-

point, but try as we may, we can never really see the world through another's eyes.

A cruel or sadistic sense of humor can be used to ridicule another individual unfairly. If the victim attempts to defend himself against these thinly veiled expressions of hostility or cruelty he may be accused of not being able to take a joke. Generally, ridicule is an abuse of the power of humor, because the victim has no socially acceptable defense, except laughter, and it is not always possible to laugh when attacked. Although it is risky to hand out insults, it is good practice to learn how to take them.

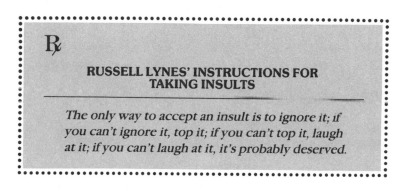

℞

RUSSELL LYNES' INSTRUCTIONS FOR TAKING INSULTS

The only way to accept an insult is to ignore it; if you can't ignore it, top it; if you can't top it, laugh at it; if you can't laugh at it, it's probably deserved.

Obviously, a jocular put-down or insult joke is superior to a direct verbal attack or overt violence. Humor is a legitimate way of discharging hostile feelings.

SOCIETY SAFETY VALVE

On special days, society eases the restraints it ordinarily places on the free expression of mirth. On New Year's Eve and April Fool's Day, for example, practical jokes and spirited behavior are more easily accepted. Private parties, reunions, festivals and certain public celebrations are frequently occasions when merrymaking and good-natured kidding around are accepted. It is desirable for a society to have these special days and functions where humor is used as a safety valve for release of social pressures.

It is bad to suppress laughter. It goes back down and spreads to your hips.

—**FRED ALLEN**

Apparently, humor has much unused potential for quelling riots or civil disturbances and for maintaining order. Humor does not produce the counterhostility and violence that suppression and police action can create. On a few occasions when demonstrations could have erupted, violence was averted by the skill of a speaker who could evoke a humorous mood.

It is a circus tradition, when something happens during a performance that might cause panic in the audience, to have the clowns come to the rescue and put on their most outrageous performance. Nonsense or irrelevant comedy performed by jugglers, acrobats and clowns has been demonstrated to be effective in reducing the pent-up anger of a hostile crowd and in averting mob violence. Avoiding violence is ultimately a contribution to solving the problem concerning the demonstrators. This in no way denies the legitimacy of the anger felt by the demonstrators or the value of their cause. Too big a head of steam can cause a blowup, leaving nothing but destruction in its wake. When tension at a public gathering or demonstration reaches a fevered pitch, the application of more pressure might be just the ingredient needed to set off an explosion. It might be better to send in the clowns than to summon the police.

HUMOR AND OUR SOCIAL ILLS

When our world comes crashing down, when a loved one disappoints us, when a trusted friend betrays that trust, when the politicians or the party we believe in is involved in scandalous behavior, when our country engages in destructive activities abroad and unconstitutional or corrupt activities at home, when law and law enforcement seems ineffective and the fabric of society seems to be unravelling before our eyes, it is faith and love and humor that provide the sustaining energy for us to carry on. In the last analysis, these seemingly fragile forces —faith, love and humor—support our conviction that life is worth living.

> *To be wildly enthusiastic, or deadly serious—both are wrong. Both pass. One must keep ever present a sense of humour. It depends entirely on yourself how much you see or hear or understand. But the sense of humour I have found of use in every single occasion of my life.*
> —KATHERINE MANSFIELD

Many of our social ills are said to be caused by the lack of a sense of community. Although this problem is complex and no simple solution is available, it would be an act of irresponsibility not to explore the potential of humor as a solution.

The book *It's a Funny Thing, Humor*, edited by Antony J. Chapman, reports an experiment in which a "humor environment" was constructed. It contained a variety of fun machinery, pictures, costumes and sound effects. Persons entering the fun environment could use any of the equipment or actually create their own humor. The study indicated that visiting the center elevated the spirits of the participants and produced other desirable mood changes. The researchers concluded that "humor environments" might be of social value to communities. This experiment may represent the wave of the future and just as for years we have tried "think tanks," maybe the time has come when we should try "laugh tanks." The creation of community-based centers in which to share in mirthmaking could be a way of breaking the barrier of isolation created by modern society.

Evidence indicates that for a community or nation to be healthy, successful and viable, it must be able to laugh at itself. This is a difficult proposition to prove, but if it is true, there is a remarkable parallel with what is known about humor and its relationship to the physical, mental and emotional health of an individual and that of a community.

> **When you make a world tolerable for yourself, you make a world tolerable for others.**
> —ANAÏS NIN

Humor plays an important role in easing the tension in interpersonal relations and it may have as useful a role to play in international relations. Although each ethnic group has a unique humor style, humor itself is universal. Humor as a unifying force has never been used systematically as official policy in international affairs. As we learn more about how to channel humor to alleviate domestic problems, it is hoped that mirth will be developed as one of the new ways of easing international tensions and communicating similarities among peoples of all nations.

PROBLEM SOLVING

What a great feeling to know that in these days of uncertainty there is at least one area of absolute certainty: When someone says to you, "No problem"... you can rest assured that there will be a problem.

THERE ARE MANY WAYS TO SOLVE A PROBLEM:

BY INVENTION

In a small town a visitor who was a devotee of archery was amazed to see a wall with ten arrows dead center in separate bull's-eyes. He approached the rather simple archer. "You're a terrific shot. How do you do it?"

"Easy. First I shoot the arrow, then I draw a big circle around it."

BY USING THE OBVIOUS

"What happened in 1898?"
"The Battleship Maine was sunk."
"What happened in 1900?"
"The Battleship Maine was sunk for two years."

BY QUICK THINKING

The boat was sinking. The skipper called out: "Does anyone know how to pray?"

"I do."

"OK, you pray," said the captain. "The rest of us will put on life belts. We're short one."

BY COMMON SENSE

FIRST COWBOY: "Why do you wear only one spur?"
SECOND COWBOY: "Wal, I figger when one side of the horse starts runnin', the other side will decide to come along."

"I'd like to buy a suit."
"Fine. First could you tell me your name, address, married or single, Democrat or Republican, and your wife's maiden name."
"Why all these questions? I only need to buy a suit."
"Ah—my friend—before we sell you a suit here, we make sure it fits your personality and position in life. We send to Australia for the proper blend of wool, from France we import just the right lining, from England, the correct buttons, then fine tailors in our shop make it fit to perfection."

"Oh—that's too bad... I need the suit tomorrow."
"You got it!"

BY ADVERTISING

When my neighbor's dog had puppies, her husband got furious with the litter underfoot. They were trying to sell the puppies, but they just weren't moving. Finally, the husband issued an ultimatum. "Advertise and get rid of these @¢*%* puppies—either they go or I go!" Soon the husband was presented with the newspaper ad: "My husband says either he goes or puppies go. Puppies are adorable, fat, pedigreed. Husband is rude, fat, mixed breed. Take your pick."

BY EVALUATION

When the family returned from church, everybody was complaining. Father didn't like the sermon. Mother didn't like the choir. The daughter said the benches were too hard.

Finally, the young son spoke up. "I don't know what all of you expected for a buck."

BY BYE

France's law of double jeopardy had just caused two prisoners to be released because the guillotine blade had malfunctioned, coming to rest inches above their necks. The third prisoner, an underachiever, mounted the stairs boldly, refused the blindfold and insisted on facing upwards toward the blade. Just as the sergeant at arms was about to call for the blade to fall, the not-too-bright prisoner said, "Wait a minute, I think I see your problem."

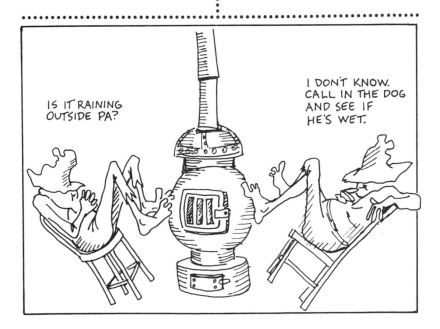

THE DEPRESSION

Earn cash in your spare time—
blackmail your friends.

•

If at first you don't succeed—
cheat!

•

An elephant is a mouse drawn
to government specifications.

•••

"The war on poverty continued
today in Washington when a
senator threw a hand grenade
at a beggar."

•

"My statistics are 100 percent
correct three percent of the
time."

•

The ABC's of Fund Raising:
  A. Persistence
  B. Persuasiveness
  C. Pistol

(Note: If you have C, you don't need
A and B.)

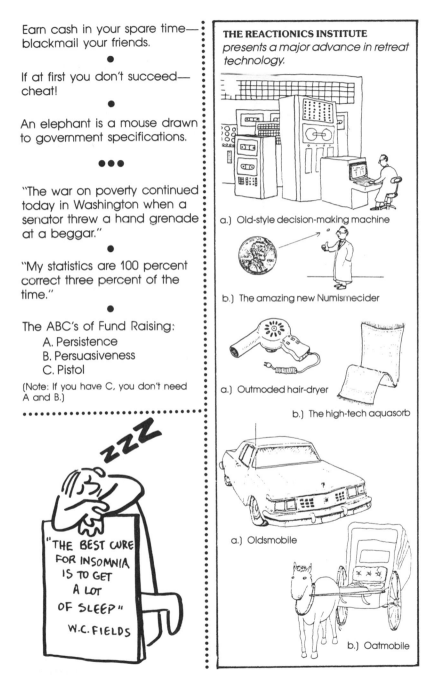

THE REACTIONICS INSTITUTE
presents a major advance in retreat technology.

a.) Old-style decision-making machine

b.) The amazing new Numismecider

a.) Outmoded hair-dryer

b.) The high-tech aquasorb

a.) Oldsmobile

b.) Oatmobile

ZZZ

"THE BEST CURE
FOR INSOMNIA
IS TO GET
A LOT
OF SLEEP"
W.C. FIELDS

GRATE EXPECTATIONS
THE FIRST PRACTICAL APPLICATION OF MURPHY'S LAW

The directions are simple. Just check the boxes according to your experience and examine the totals. If the miracle occurs that the number of checks in the DIDN'T HAPPEN column add up to more than the number of checks in the HAPPENED column, you have every right to rejoice and feel secure that things are starting to go your way. If, however, the number of checks in the DIDN'T HAPPEN column are less than in the HAPPENED column, no sweat, you are already an expert in handling your everyday disasters.

FLIGHT NUMBER 631 FINAL CALL DEPARTING GATE ONE !!!

GATE 359   GATE 358

GRATE EXPECTATIONS OF AIR TRAVEL

	YOU EXPECTED IT TO HAPPEN, IT HAPPENED.	YOU EXPECTED IT TO HAPPEN, IT **DIDN'T** HAPPEN!
1. You defy the traffic laws to arrive on time. The "on time" departure will be an hour late.	☐	☐
2. The type of airplane you're flying will have made unfortunate headlines recently.	☐	☐
3. Your departure gate will always be the farthest from the terminal, regardless of its number.	☐	☐
4. You will hear someone ask, "How can they get a big thing like this off the ground?"	☐	☐
5. The plane will not shake until the meal is served.	☐	☐
6. The amount of turbulence will be in direct proportion to the heat of your coffee.	☐	☐
7. The person next to you will either be a white knuckler or will have a need for the little white bag.	☐	☐
8. You will be seated next to a crying baby.	☐	☐
9. When you finally get to use the lavatory, the "Return to Your Seat" sign will go on.	☐	☐
10. On a short flight, your food and your destination will arrive at the same time.	☐	☐
TOTAL		

IF THIS AMOUNT IS GREATER: THINGS ARE LOOKING UP! If smaller: So what else is new?

.... **PROBLEM-SOLVING PRODUCTS** ....

Do you have that terrible itching feeling?
Do what millions of Americans do.
Try...

Sweating?
Smelling bad?
Friends giving you lots of leeway?
Start your way back to social acceptance....
Resort to...

Hung over?
We know the feeling.
That's why our company offers an
    after-excess miracle:

Having nasal stuffiness?
That clogged-up feeling?
Maybe it's time to...

Is your cigarette just laying there?
Would you love to smoke it?
Could it be that you need...

Revolutionary cure for boredom!
It's simple!
It's affordable!
Read...

Not getting enough fun out of life?
Nagging bills piling up?
Miss that vacation you used to take?
Maybe you need...

Hungry?
Maybe even starved?
Why not...

Head aching?
Do you have that pounding
of the skull?
Why not take...

PROBLEM-SOLVING DEVICES

If you are a football/baseball/basketball or other widow or widower—have the object of your defection take this simple test.

TUBE JOCK AWARENESS TEST

	YES	NO
Do you have a fierce pride based on territorial imperative, civic and/or local allegiance for your team?	☐	☐
Do you understand that practically no member of the team is from your territory, city or locality?	☐	☐
Do you comprehend that the players are mercenaries, playing for the team that pays them the most money and gives them the most "incentives"?	☐	☐
Are you aware of the fact that any player would leave your team in 9.2 seconds flat for a better offer?	☐	☐
Do you understand any more than the mere basics of the game?	☐	☐
Do you realize that the smartest, most astute team owner's motto is "It is not whether you win or lose, but what the paid attendance was"?	☐	☐

	YES	NO
Do you spend more time watching the sporting event than reading a good book?	☐	☐
More time than exercising?	☐	☐
More time than checking in with the family?	☐	☐
More time than having sex?	☐	☐
Do you realize that the money spent on professional sports exceeds our investment in the cure for cancer?	☐	☐
Do you not recognize a strange injustice in the fact that athletes should earn ten to twenty times more than professors, scientists, doctors and the President of the United States?	☐	☐
Does it bother you that the loyal fans who have sweated and frozen through the season cannot get into the park during the World Series or Super Bowl time?	☐	☐
Don't you feel hypocritical because the ethnic you cheer on the field is from a race about which you have much different feelings off the field?	☐	☐
Do you realize that the term "jock" is derived from a protective garment worn about the male genitalia?	☐	☐

Kindly complete and return before our relationship continues.

· ·

"I'm sorry, I can't give you a room. We're all booked up for tonight."
"If the President of the United States came in would you have a room for him?"
"Of course. Certainly, we would."
"Well, I got news for you—he's not com ing. So, I'll take his room!"

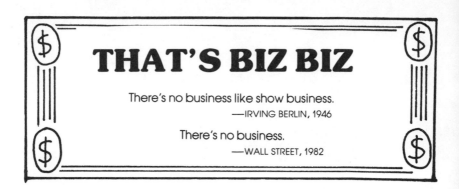

THAT'S BIZ BIZ

There's no business like show business.
—IRVING BERLIN, 1946

There's no business.
—WALL STREET, 1982

A manufacturer sending a letter to a client who owes an outstanding bill for goods—

Dear Mr. Levy:
After checking our records, we note that we have done more for you than your own mother did. We carried you for fifteen months.

• • •

A salesman held over in Hawaii by a tropical storm wired his firm:
MAROONED BY STORM. SEND INSTRUCTIONS.

His firm replied:
START VACATION AS OF YESTERDAY.

• • •

A brain is an organ that starts working the moment you get up in the morning and does not stop until you get into the office.
—ROBERT FROST

"The sign painters are on strike."

SHOE REPAIR

I FOUND THIS TICKET FROM 1978...

SHOE REPAIR

I DON'T SUPPOSE YOU'LL STILL HAVE THEM...

SHOE REPAIR

THEY'LL BE READY ON THURSDAY.

The president of a company addressed the employees of the plant.

PRESIDENT:
I know you've all heard that we're going to be automated and you're worried that these robots will take over your jobs. Well, I'm happy to tell you that not only will no one be let go, but you will only be required to come to work *one* day a week for a full week's pay. That's right, you'll only have to work on Wednesdays!

From the back came the voice of an employee.

EMPLOYEE:
Every Wednesday?

• • •

SECRETARY:
Boss, I've got good news and bad news.

BOSS:
Give me the good news first.

SECRETARY:
You're not sterile.

I CAN'T APPROVE YOUR EXPENSE ACCOUNT BUT I WOULD LIKE TO BUY THE FICTION RIGHTS.

"I just heard Phil died."
"What did he have?"
"Nothing much... a few small accounts—nothing worth going after."

Sign on the plant manager's door:

IF YOU HAVE PROBLEMS, COME IN AND TELL ME ABOUT THEM. IF YOU DON'T, COME IN AND TELL ME HOW YOU DO IT.

"You don't have to take that, you know!"

"Where is the manager's office?"

"Take the elevator that says 'Out of Order.' Then go past the sign that says 'No Admittance' and through the door that says 'For Emergency Use Only'... then holler for him."

Stunned by the beauty of their new secretary, two executives resolved to make her adjustment to the firm their business.

"It's up to us to teach her the difference between what's right and what's wrong," said one.

"Absolutely," said the other. "You teach her what's right."

• • •

Bankruptcy: When you put your money in your pants pocket and give your coat to your creditors.
—PAUL STEINER

•

Office Axiom: The boss will be late when you are early and early when you are late.

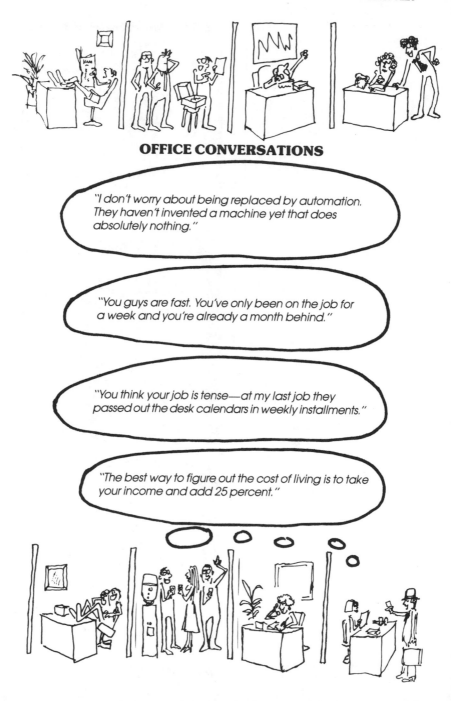

OFFICE CONVERSATIONS

"I don't worry about being replaced by automation. They haven't invented a machine yet that does absolutely nothing."

"You guys are fast. You've only been on the job for a week and you're already a month behind."

"You think your job is tense—at my last job they passed out the desk calendars in weekly installments."

"The best way to figure out the cost of living is to take your income and add 25 percent."

You need a job to pay those hospital bills . . . But you must pay the bills before they'll discharge you? Now you can beat that CRUTCH-22 by

Exciting temporary careers for the temporarily handicapped.*

············· ★ SAMPLE OPPORTUNITIES ★ ···············

SMOKE ALARM: Some family can rest secure because you're hanging around.

OUTDOOR ADVERTISING:
Be a Boo Boo Board

*Research scientists: Stanley M. Miller & Evelyn S. Dana

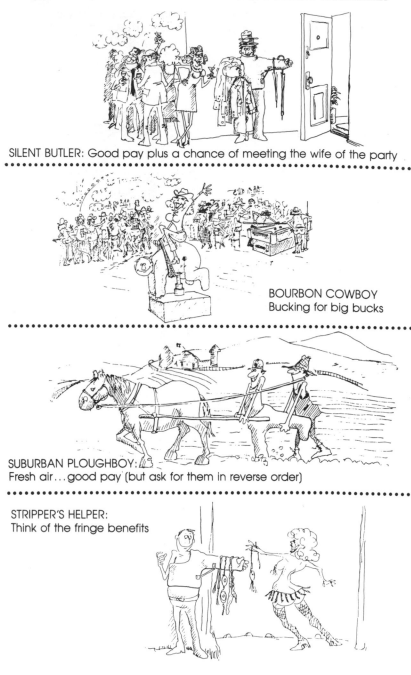

SILENT BUTLER: Good pay plus a chance of meeting the wife of the party

BOURBON COWBOY
Bucking for big bucks

SUBURBAN PLOUGHBOY:
Fresh air...good pay (but ask for them in reverse order)

STRIPPER'S HELPER:
Think of the fringe benefits

PLANTER'S AIDE:
On the hole,
a good job

BE A 100% ACCURATE T.V. WEATHERMAN:
1. Face camera.
2. Place cast out window.
3. If cast is wet—predict rain.
   If cast is warm—predict sunshine.

WEDDING ATTENDANT:
Requires a background in
Marital Arts

PLACE KICKER:
The thrill of victory
from the agony of
the feet

MINING:
Your own business

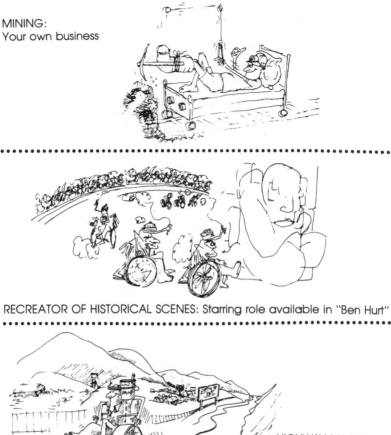

RECREATOR OF HISTORICAL SCENES: Starring role available in "Ben Hurt"

HIGHWAY MARKER:
The perfect answer
to "What's your line?"

SMUGGLER:
Not for the meek or those
afraid of being busted

BOO BOO BOARD # 2

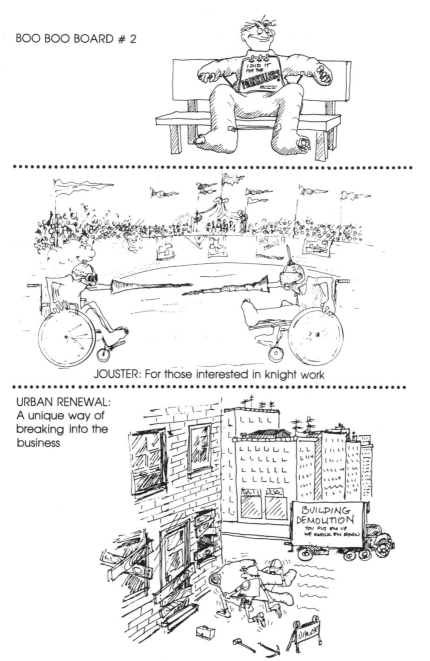

JOUSTER: For those interested in knight work

URBAN RENEWAL:
A unique way of
breaking into the
business

PUTDOWNS©

• •

Just put down the appropriate name and safely get the venom out of your system.

_____ doesn't know the meaning of the word defeat... and several thousand other words.

_____ locked himself/herself in the car and broke a window to get out.

_____ turned a few heads in his/her day—and a few stomachs too.

_____ 's face could stop a calendar.

Yesterday _____ was arrested for "mooning," and they found out it was his/her face.

_____ 's face looks like it was used to test golf shoes.

_____ couldn't lure a man/woman out of a burning building.

Plastic surgeons have to fix _____ 's face before it's condemned.

The wart on _____ 's face is his/her best feature.

_____ talks so much he/she could open a branch mouth.

When _____ goes to the zoo, elephants throw peanuts at him/her.

_____ is on the critical list at Weight Watchers.

_____ is so mean ...he/she throws a beer party and then locks the bathroom.

I don't know what makes _____ so obnoxious, but whatever it is...it works.

_____ was invited to a séance. No one would hold his/her hand.

Saying nice things about _____ is like coming out on behalf of athlete's foot.

_____ is so old that his/her blood type was discontinued.

_____ should put a quarter under his/her pillow for the gum fairy.

_____ has seen better days. In fact, he's/she's seen better decades.

_____ fries his bacon in Woolite so it won't shrink.

* *The Hostility Handbook*, Bill Dana, Simon & Schuster, New York, 1982

_____ has all the charm of World War Three.

May a pregnant elephant sit on _____ 's car keys.

May an eighty-year-old onion farmer give _____ mouth-to-mouth resuscitation.

May the toothpick _____ puts in his/her mouth have Dutch elm disease.

May the ringing in _____ 's ears be a wrong number.

May _____ ask a mean waitress for a side order of preservatives in a health food restaurant.

May _____ get a vapor lock in his/her pacemaker.

May _____ inherit three hundred Marcel Marceau records.

May _____ marry the boss's ugly daughter, then discover that the company is bankrupt.

_____ is so dull he/she couldn't stand out in a crowd if he/she hung around with the seven dwarfs.

_____ has no equals . . . superiors, yes.

_____ is such a slob that when he/she hung his/her stocking on the Xmas tree, the tree died.

_____ is as useful as an ashtray on a motorcycle.

If their son _____ was their only child he still wouldn't be their favorite.

Someday _____ is going to find himself/herself and he's/she's going to be disappointed.

_____ wears industrial strength dress shields.

_____ 's toupee makes him look twenty years sillier.

_____ 's cooking is so bad even the garbage disposal rejected it.

THE DR. LAURENCE PETER
COMPETENCY
ANALYSIS

Knowing thyself is the key to competency. Test #1 helps you analyze your thought processes and Test #2 assists you in evaluating the state of your mental health.

• •

TEST 1.
PROVERB APTITUDE TEST—PAT

Personal beliefs are important to your way of life. To get a better understanding of your own beliefs, prejudices and idiosyncracies, identify the following proverbs as either True (T) or False (F).

1. Look before you leap.   T   F
   He who hesitates is lost.   T   F

2. If at first you don't succeed, try, try again.   T   F
   Once bitten, twice shy.   T   F

3. You can't teach an old dog new tricks.   T   F
   It's never too late to learn.   T   F

4. Where there's a will, there's a way.   T   F
   Time and tide wait for no man.   T   F

5. Out of sight, out of mind.   T   F
   Absence makes the heart grow fonder.   T   F

6. Two heads are better than one.   T   F
   If you want something done right, do it yourself.   T   F

7. Never look a gift horse in the mouth.   T   F
   All that glitters is not gold.   T   F

8. You can't tell a book by its cover.   T   F
   Clothes make the man.   T   F

9. Many hands make light work.   T   F
   Too many cooks spoil the broth.   T   F

10. Better safe than sorry.   T   F
    Nothing ventured, nothing gained.   T   F

TEST 2.
HEALTH OF MIND EXAMINATION—HOME

In evaluating your mental health, select and circle the statement that best describes YOU.

1. Do you suffer from indecision?
   A. yes
   B. no
   C. maybe
2. Are you too independent?
   A. go to hell
   B. that is impossible
   C. does not apply
3. Are you too dependent?
   A. I'll have to ask my wife
   B. I'll have to ask my husband
   C. I'll have to ask my mother
4. If at first you don't succeed
   A. try, try again
   B. change your tactics
   C. forget it
5. When driving a car you should
   A. read all signs and ignore the road
   B. watch the road and ignore the signs
   C. watch the people and ignore the road and the signs

● ●

SCORING:

TEST 1. PROVERB APTITUDE TEST—PAT: 1 point for each correct answer.

1. F	3. F	5. F	7. F	9. F
2. F	4. F	6. F	8. F	10. F

TEST 2. HEALTH OF MIND EXAMINATION—HOME: Responses to these questions place you in one of three categories:

A. POSITIVE THINKER If you persisted in trying to answer these silly questions, you are a positive thinker and are destined to a frustrating existence in which you habitually attempt the impossible.

B. NEGATIVE THINKER If you gave up quickly, you are a negative thinker and are destined to attain adequate rest and sleep.

C. RIGHT THINKER If you turned directly to SCORING to find the answers, you are a right thinker and are destined to a life of efficiency in which you do not waste time doing things the hard way.

12.

Learn Eloquence the Easy Way

●●

1. Become an effective communicator through studying at home.
2. Win friends through your witty conversation.
3. Increase your influence and income by becoming a creative, confident and competent public speaker.

BOOKS

Meta-Talk: Guide to Hidden Meanings in Conversation, Gerard I. Nierenberg and Henry Calero. Trident Press, New York, 1973.

The reader of this book will be sensitized to the unconscious meanings and motivations that threaten to distort dialogue and cause misunderstandings. He/she will discover that, curiously, the emptiest and most routine everyday phrases are the ones that prove richest in subliminal significance. Although the term "meta-talk" is

new, the idea it represents has been around for a long time. The authors of this book recount the research on subverbal communication by psychologists, general semanticists and others, from Aristotle to Freud to present-day researchers.

How To Talk with Practically Anybody about Practically Anything. Barbara Walters. Doubleday and Co., Inc., New York, 1970.

The author, a leading television interviewer, provides sample interviews and anecdotes about the famous persons she has met. Most individuals respond favorably to pleasant personal questions if they reflect genuine interest in the person. Each individual has experiences that will be of interest if we can get the individual to talk about them.

Instant Eloquence: A Lazy Man's Guide to Public Speaking, James C. Humes. Harper and Row, Publishers, New York, 1973.

In this practical handbook, the author, an experienced public speaker and speech writer, shows how to prepare a speech quickly and easily for almost any occasion. The book illustrates how to open a speech, research and plan a message and end on a high note. Included are suggestions on how to have yourself introduced, how to handle hecklers and how to establish rapport with your audience. One thousand and three hundred sayings, quotations and stories help highlight points you might wish to make.

Orben's Current Comedy, Robert Orben, editor. The Comedy Center, 700 Orange Street, Wilmington, Delaware 19801.

Current Comedy consists of four pages of jokes and one-liners. It contains material for speakers and toastmasters along with quips for handling hecklers. Much of the material is based on current events. It is sent by first-class mail twice each month to subscribers.

Understanding Laughter: The Workings of Wit and Humor, Charles R. Gruner, Ph.D. Nelson-Hall Publishers, Chicago, 1979.

The author, a professor of speech communication at the University of Georgia, has studied the effect of humor on communication and has conducted many experiments to test the validity of his findings. In this book, he offers a collection of humorous material, theories and explanations of why we laugh and illustrations of how wit and humor can catch the attention of an audience. The book closes with a social and psychological analysis of the contribution wit and humor can make to persuasive speeches.

Peter's Quotations: Ideas for Our Time, Laurence J. Peter, William Morrow and Company, Inc., New York, 1977.

This is a reference book that is fun to read—an idea mine for writers, students and lecturers— with gems of brevity, wit and originality relevant to the problems of today. The focus is on ideas rather than words, and there are many unusual and little-known quotations of great wit. The book has a name and author index as well as a table of subjects completely cross-referenced by related categories.

It's a Funny Thing, Humor, Antony J. Chapman, editor. Pergamon Press, New York, 1977.

The research report, "Laughter in the Basement," included in this book, describes how a group of behavioral scientists designed, built and tested the effects of a "humor environment." They equipped this environment with a wide variety of fun machinery for visitors' entertainment. Jokes and cartoons were on display. Costumes and masks were readily available. Toys and gadgets, as well as creative outlets for expressions of humor, were provided. Visitors, encouraged to engage in any activity they liked, were observed constantly through one-way mirrors, and their actions were recorded by a hidden television camera. Standard psychological tests of each person's mood were given before and following each visit to the humor area. The results reveal that the environment was effective in elevating the spirits of the individuals. The report writers conclude that such centers might be of social value to communities because it appears that mirth promotes social harmony.

AUDIO TAPES

For those interested in becoming effective public speakers, there are a number of high-quality courses available on tape. There are also single tapes of advice and illustration to help the listener improve communication skills.

Communicating What You Think, Earl Nightingale. Write: Nightingale-Conant Corporation, 3730 West Devon Avenue, Chicago, Illinois 60659.

Earl Nightingale presents this twenty-lesson program on six cassette tapes. It is a basic, practical guide to successful communication. Contents: *Speaking with Strength and Effectiveness*; *Creating the Message*; *One Idea at a Time*; *Don't Underestimate Your Audience*; *Aim and Hang Loose*; *Speak in the Language of Your Listeners*; *Keep Things in Order*; *Preparing a Talk*; *Visual Aids*; *No Small Parts*; *Stay Attuned for Feedback*; *Who Do You Think You're Talking To?*; *Like Your Audience*; *Controlled Relaxation*; *Keep it Clear*; *Speak from the Other Side*; *But Are They Buying?*; *On Playing Tennis*; *On Preparing a Meeting*; *How to Make a Speech*.

The Compleat Speaker, Earl Nightingale. Write: Nightingale-Conant Corporation, 3730 West Devon Avenue, Chicago, Illinois 60659.

In this course, Earl Nightingale offers a more advanced and comprehensive six-cassette program covering a wide range of public speaking situations. It includes delivering extemporaneous remarks; introductions; moderating panels; interviews and more. Contents: *Preamble*; *A Review of the Basics*; *Outlining a Speech*; *On Writing a Speech*; *Speaking with Style*; *An Informative Speech*; *A Convincing Speech*; *The Inspiring Speech*; *Using Humor in a Speech*; *Motivating the Audience*; *The Impromptu Speech*; *Special Occasions*; *Intro's, Awards, Etc.*; *Include the Visual Dimension*; *Reading a Speech*; *Watch Your Words*; *Moderating a Panel*; *Handling Conflict Situations*; *Radio and Television Interviews*; *Communicating on the Telephone*; *Communicating in a Meeting*.

Effective Speaking for Managers, Robert L. Montgomery. Write: Amacon, 135 West 50 Street, New York, New York 10020.

In this course, produced by a division of the American Management Association, Robert L. Montgomery presents a four-hour program designed to improve communication skills: to help you communicate with individuals, be effective in meetings, improve as a platform speaker, increase confidence, motivate others and provide leadership.

Communicating Skills. Write: Addison-Wesley Publishing Co., Reading, Massachusetts 01867.

This set of six short (ten- to fifteen-minute) tapes covers "do's and don'ts" in communication and includes advice on correcting or avoiding common problems.

Speech Training Tapes. Write: Bureau of Business Practice, 24 Rope Ferry Road, Waterford, Connecticut 06385.

These twelve talks are aimed at improving self-expression skills. Topics covered include: the humorous speech, opening and closing with humor, overcoming stage fright, audience involvement, building enthusiasm, persuasion, proper delivery, the climax, visual aids and speaking extemporaneously.

The Art of Public Speaking, Mildred Bennet. Write: Success Motivation Institute, P.O. Box 7614, Waco, Texas 76710.

On this cassette, Mildred Bennet shows how to get your ideas accepted by others. She goes beyond the act of public speaking to include points on leadership and how to attain security, peace of mind and a happy life.

The Comedy of Love, Dr. Herb True. Write: Success Motivation Institute, P.O. Box 7614, Waco, Texas 76710.

Dr. Herb True presents thought-provoking ideas about love and its many forms. This tape is useful as an example of the value of humor in communicating important ideas.

PART IV

Do It Yourself

●●●

Create Your Own Humor

13.

Develop Your Sense of Humor

●●●

A sense of humor keen enough to show a man his own absurdities as well as those of other people will keep a man from commission of all sins, or nearly all, save those that are worth committing.

—SAMUEL BUTLER

Humans have tried to understand why they laugh for as long as they have sought to understand their own nature. Written explanations of humor go back at least as far as the early Greeks. Many studies deal with the history and development of humor, and theories of humor abound. Interesting though these studies may be academically, they are of little practical value.

Defining and analyzing humor is a pastime of humorless people.

—ROBERT BENCHLEY

A sense of humor is a many-splendored thing. It involves everything in this book and much more. A sense of humor gives you the ability to (1) relax so that your objectivity can help you see the inconsistencies in your own behavior and the incongruities in the human condition, (2) resolve problems, (3) laugh at illness and trouble, (4) create your own mirth and (5) communicate effectively. A sense of humor has these specific applications and more generally, can help shape an attitude, a humorous outlook on life.

> *Human life is basically a comedy. Even its tragedies often seem comic to the spectator, and not infrequently they actually have comic touches to the victim. Happiness probably consists largely in the capacity to detect and relish them.*
>
> —H.L. MENCKEN

Everybody laughs at something. Even an adult who appears humorless laughed as a child. The infant laughed when tickled and the child laughed when engaged in play. As we mature, our senses of humor develop as individualistically as do all our other personal characteristics.

The total concept we call a sense of humor has many levels —from the laughter elicited by the antics of a clown to the more abstract and complex ideas involved in a humorous perception of life. Because an individual may respond to humor at one level and not at another, our discussion of the development of a sense of humor will begin with a look at the levels of response: (1) the Audience Level, (2) the Situational Level, (3) the Other Person Level, (4) the Self Level, and (5) the Perspective Level.

THE AUDIENCE LEVEL

When we attend a comedy performance, our sense of humor causes us to respond with laughter or amusement to the presentation. Jokes, skits and comic plays are written so that we will laugh at certain intervals. In slapstick comedy, the pratfall, pie in the face or other sight gag signals our laughter. Since laughter is contagious, if a substantial number laugh, nearly everyone in the audience will laugh. In vaudeville, the comic storyteller or comedian developed techniques to enhance the response to his presentation by signalling the audience when to laugh. Each punchline was accompanied by a rim shot by the drummer, a funny facial expression, a flick of a cigar or some other gesture. This technique has had its ultimate application in television comedy. Initially, because the viewer was at home, the audience contagion effect was lacking. This was resolved by using a studio audience whose laughter drew in the home viewer. To assure that the studio audience would laugh at the correct places in the script during the actual performance, a warm-up period was provided in which the audience was rehearsed in laughing on cue. In cases where this technique did not produce enough laughter it was considered necessary to augment the audience laughter with canned laughter from a laugh machine. Some comedy series were produced in segments without an audience. These segments were assembled at a later date, with the machine contributing all the laughter at the places indicated in the script.

> *I find television very educating. Every time somebody turns on the set I go into the other room and read a book.*
>
> —GROUCHO MARX

Reading humorous material is a special case at the audience level. One is often amused at what one reads but only occasionally does one laugh out loud as one would at a performance of the same material. The tendency to laugh at written material usually occurs when it produces strong visual imagery.

A sense of humor gives you the ability to respond to something contrived to amuse you: a humorous book, a joke told by a friend, a movie or TV program, a comedy performance, or simply a conditioned response created through the advanced technology of television.

> *Pure drivel tends to drive ordinary drivel off the TV screen.*
>
> —MARVIN KITMAN

THE SITUATIONAL LEVEL

When you are able to see humor in everyday events, you are deriving humor from situations not designed to produce laughter. When someone mistakes the horseradish for sour cream and is surprised when he bites into his baked potato, we may laugh. The accident has caused the victim shock but only mild discomfort and no serious injury. The situation is similar to much of the comedy we see on stage. The only difference is that as members of an audience we know we are expected to laugh, and in the real life situation we may not be sure.

In the development of a sense of humor your role as audience primes you to appreciate humor at higher levels. In the movie *The Bank Dick*, W. C. Fields plays the part of a shiftless braggart with a prodigious thirst for hard liquor. Purely by accident, he trips an escaping bank robber and becomes a hero. Without mending his ways in the slightest, he moves from being the butt of the town's jokes to being one of its most successful and respected citizens. Many viewers, laughing at this great comedy, see parallels between the movie and situations in the real world. This contributes to their ability to see the irony when they witness honors for good citizenship being bestowed on business-people well known for their ruthless practices or humanitarian awards being presented to entertainers with well-established underworld connections.

THE OTHER PERSON LEVEL

Laughing at others' mistakes, problems, handicaps, misfortunes or idiosyncrasies is similar to laughing at a situation comedy, in that you are laughing at something or someone outside yourself. If the other person sees the humor in his situation or his behavior, your laughter is shared and it becomes "laughing with" rather than "laughing at" the individual.

> *Everything is funny as long as it is happening to somebody else.*
>
> —WILL ROGERS

THE SELF LEVEL

There is general agreement that the ability to laugh at yourself, at your own appearance, flaws and foolishness, is the ultimate in humor. Laughing at yourself is beneficial when it is done with affection and tolerance—that is, when you perceive yourself as flawed and silly, but basically lovable. When we view others as imperfect but lovable there is greater probability that we will see ourselves reflected in them and therefore see ourselves as laughable. Laughing at yourself is destructive only when you mock yourself in self-hatred or bitterness. When we laugh at ourselves with affection, while recognizing our imperfections and idiosyncrasies, we achieve a state of humility in which we accept ourselves as worthy of esteem but not in need of unquestioned adulation. Viewing yourself with humor is the most effective antidote for the tendency to be vain and self-righteous.

Every time we laugh at our own stupid selves, we
reinforce our feeling for the ludicrous. We reinforce
and expand it in its most essential realm, for we remind
ourselves that foolishness, like charity, begins at home.
—HARVEY MINDESS

THE PERSPECTIVE LEVEL

The ability to see the funny side of things, to appreciate the ridiculous in life and to laugh at our troubles is one of the greatest assets one can possess. A humorous perspective includes all four levels of humorous response described above and goes beyond them to embrace a whole way of looking at life. Like love, compassion, understanding and courage, a humorous attitude can help sustain us through good times and bad. It can lighten the load of our daily routine and responsibilities. It can help us through suffering and pain, and it even can enable us to live joyous lives in the worst of times. The humorous perspective is fundamental to complete mental health. Research that focuses on the relationship between a sense of humor and mental health supports the view that humor is an important component of healthy mental and emotional adjustment. The level of an individual's humor appreciation is an indication of one's degree of mental maturity and emotional health. Conversely, lack of humor, or a limited reaction to humor, is an indicator of inhibition or a restrictive life style. The humorous perspective is the ultimate achievement in the quest for happiness and good mental health.

The only thing worth having in an earthly existence is
a sense of humor.
—LINCOLN STEFFENS

You will survive almost any emotional problem if you have a humorous perspective—your own humorous climate, or tone, for living. Once you achieve the habit of looking on the bright side, you will find it easier to cut problems down to manageable size.

If you have been in the habit of looking on the dark side, and you have difficulty finding humorous situations or feel you have been missing some of the joy and laughter life can provide, here is a way to a new beginning. Start a collection of happy and humorous memories. Reminisce about the happy incidents of your childhood. Remember the amusing things that happened at home and at school. Recall the pranks your co-workers played or funny things that occurred. Include any experience that made you laugh or feel good, whether it was an anecdote that someone told, a happy circumstance, or a comical event. Making a list of these cherished happenings is a useful activity. Keep looking for funny experiences to add to your list. Include jokes and stories that you find particularly amusing. Look for constructive and positive humor, which you will find, in the long run, to be more rewarding than anti-ethnic or put-down humor. Return to your list frequently and enjoy recalling the happy times. Tell your funny experiences to your friends, so they will want to share more joy with you, thus multiplying the laughs for everyone. The triggering of laughter in others and their sharing in your experiences facilitates the development of a humorous group perspective—the feeling that we all can laugh at ourselves and at each other's failings and that we hold amusing experiences in common in this mad world.

The five levels at which we respond to humor range from simple to complex; from simple responsiveness to a complex frame of mind. Because these levels form a gradation they can be used as a guide in development of a sense of humor. They can be the steps that lead to the accomplishment of a fully developed sense of humor.

In order to laugh or appreciate the humor of a situation, one often has to suspend a sense of the immediate. Acquiring a sense of humor involves developing a mental mechanism whereby you are able to achieve a level of conscious or unconscious mental or emotional awareness that allows a temporary escape. This escape alleviates a painful or overwhelming reality with which the individual otherwise cannot cope.

This temporary period of relief, when reality is held in abeyance, is sometimes referred to as mild regression, for in a way it is a return to a type of fantasy that we frequently believe we have outgrown. But, it is this playfulness or childishness that facilitates the suspension of reality and the creation of fantasy that leads to problem solving.

> *It seems to me people are often sympathetic when they laugh. Take this dog we're working on. He has swallowed a magnet, and he gets in an awful predicament. All the kitchen knives jump out of the drawer when he comes by and go after him. People laugh, but I think they sympathize with the dog. They are glad, not sorry, when he gets out of his trouble. Sometimes little children sympathize too much, and have to shut their eyes during a cruel scene.*
>
> —WALT DISNEY

A vital sense of humor is based on an ability to cut loose from our customary mode of thinking. It is the ability to be playful with that which customarily is thought to be serious. A fully functioning sense of humor must be iconoclastic, impulsive, irreverent and impertinent. We must delight in being uninhibited. Take any conventional conduct and visualize the most unconventional or contradictory behavior and you have the essence of humor. Take the most accepted thought and then give it the most unconventional treatment and you have created humor.

Humor is release from that which is normal or conventional. It is the escape from the conventional that is funny. We must be able to see what is socially acceptable before we can see what is humorous. Having a sense of humor means seeing the incongruity between what we profess to be and what we really are.

> *Wit is the sudden marriage of ideas which before their marriage were not perceived to have any relationship.*
>
> —MARK TWAIN

At its highest level, a sense of humor is the ability both to appreciate and to poke fun at every side of every belief, argument or proposal, including your own. This does not mean that you are complacent about bigotry, injustice, hypocrisy or violence, but that you have a humorous perspective on life.

In order to fully embrace life and accept ourselves, we must be realistic about ourselves and about our world. We might wish the human race were better and that we were wonderful, but we must live with reality. You can still believe in the improvement of the human condition even if you don't believe in its perfection.

> *You grow up the day you have your first real laugh—at yourself.*
>
> —ETHEL BARRYMORE

Most helpful humor involves the good-natured contemplation of life's incongruities. One can perceive life's paradoxes and respond either with anger and violence or with humor. Therefore, we must conclude that humor is more than the ability to see our pretensions, contradictions and deceits. It is the ability to perceive these paradoxes from a position of emotional distance. To see the humor in a situation we must have sufficient impulse control to not respond with immediate overt hostility. We must be able to see the incongruity with enough objectivity and tolerance so that our emotions do not get out of hand. Nearly anyone can respond with humor in retrospect. We sometimes can laugh later about an annoying or upsetting situation that at the time caused an emotional outburst. A highly effective sense of humor can help us view the present annoyance in a similar manner to the way we will view it sometime in the future.

For those interested in further study, the most informative book I have found on the subject of developing your sense of humor is *Laughter and Liberation* by Harvey Mindess, a psychotherapist who teaches courses on the uses of humor.

℞

PETER'S PRESCRIPTION FOR DEVELOPMENT OF YOUR SENSE OF HUMOR

1. *Adopt an attitude of playfulness. This does not mean that you will do outrageous things, but that your mind is open to uncensored, iconoclastic, silly or outrageous thoughts.*
2. *Think funny. See the funny side or flip side of every situation. Select and refine your outrageous thoughts that best expose our conceits, pomposities and incongruities.*
3. *Laugh at the incongruities in situations involving yourself and others.*
4. *Only laugh with others for what they do rather than for what they are, unless you are assured that they can laugh at themselves for what they are. In laughing with others about their incongruities, see them as mirrors in which your own weaknesses, idiosyncrasies and conceits are reflected.*
5. *Laugh at yourself, not in derision, but with objectivity and acceptance of self.*
6. *Take yourself lightly. Take your job and your responsibility to yourself and to others seriously. You will discover that this will make life's anxieties and burdens lighter.*
7. *Make others laugh. By creating happiness for others, you will experience a special joy of accomplishment that only a lively, generous sense of humor can bring.*
8. *Realize that a sense of humor is deeper than laughter and more satisfactory than comedy, and delivers greater rewards than merely being entertaining. A sense of humor sees the fun in everyday experiences. It is more important to have fun than it is to be funny.*

PUMPING IRONY

HUMOROBICS • JESTING-UP EXERCISES
PREMISES-PREMISES

If the same people who create the cutie-pie, artsy-craftsy names for shops like: Hairdresser—RAPE OF THE LOCKS, were given the job of naming the world's most imposing and famous edifices, the result might be as follows:

> The Pentagon: BOMBS R US
> The Kremlin: THE COMRADE HILTON
> The Sistine Chapel: STAY 'N' PRAY
> Stratford-Upon-Avon Hotel: BED 'N' BARD
> The Bastille: LE SLAMMEUR
> The Supreme Court: DECISIONS, DECISIONS

Examine some samples from our punabridged dictionary. Then see if you can get wit it.

A hip snake ....A smart asp
Ticked-off simians ....The Apes of Wrath
Funny puckers ....Lip Schtick
Unknown dog..Anonymut
To make someone die laughing............................Humorcide
Big nudist laugh..Buffola
Protective garment worn as a necktie....................Jerk strap
Decorum in Russia ....Sovietiquette
That feeling of almost joy ....Perhappiness
Command performance at the White House ....Presidentertainment
Thirteen-year-old smoker..................................Nicoteenager
Your uncle in the clothing business.......................Apparelative
Hare Krishnas at Hungarian airport.......................Bhudda Pest
A dumb water carrier ....Gunga Dim
Disagreement in sportscar ....Jaguargument

• •

To develop your body muscles, play with rackets, bats and balls.
To develop your mental muscles...

PLAY WITH WORDS

DEF (IN·IT) IONS

HOW TO PLAY:

Find the smaller word inside the big word which relates to the clue.

SAMPLE:

A second-class midget   U N IMP O R T A N T

  (A second-class midget is an Unimportant Imp)

Taking pictures of clothing   P H O TOG R A P H Y

  (Taking pictures of clothing is Tog Photography)

A TV or radio commercial   B R O AD C A S T

  (A TV or radio commercial is a Broadcast Ad)

• •

Joy in being together	RELATIONSHIP
Unemployed young lady	DISMISSED
Definitely an old stringed instrument	ABSOLUTELY
Remembering Muhammed	IMMORTALIZED
A ripped attorney	ATTORNEY
A tremendous berg	MAGNIFICENT
The young marrieds upstairs	COUPLE
Bad in Brazil	NOTORIOUS
A group of air conditioning salesmen	CONVENTION
Acknowledge the kid's birthday	CELEBRATE
An angry display	FIREWORKS
Anger at congressman	REPRESENTATIVE
Farmer's groupies	AGRICULTURE
Observations about males	COMMENTARY
Tabby's time off	VACATION
Going to the same delicatessen	FIDELITY
An erupting soup container	VOLCANO
Tardy adjustment	MANIPULATE
Rope inventory	RECORDING
On behalf of the Golden State	CALIFORNIA

Giving on the Q.T.	GENEROUSLY
The G.O.P. bar in London	REPUBLICAN
They just fade away	SOLDIERS
To tell with happiness	RELATE
Defense from decay	PROTECTION
Openly sneaky	OBVIOUSLY
Staff of jewelry store	MANAGEMENT
Advertisement for spy	COMMERCIAL
Relaxing combatant	WRESTLER
Upright browning	STANDING
Hitting on males	HARASSMENT
Daddy's coming	ANTICIPATE
Unsuccessful track circling	COLLAPSED
Finding blanket	DISCOVERY
Annoying decaying metal	FRUSTRATED
Guessers of gold	THEORETICIANS
Prohibit lust	ABANDON
Mickey the pervert	ABERRATION
Trying to be like your boy	IMPERSONATION
Y.M.C.A.	ESTABLISHMENT
Porch builder	OCCUPATION
Headgear for any occasion	WHATEVER
President of knife company	EXECUTIVE

Sometimes The Funniest Things Are Said In Jest

GOT A MATCH?

1. Three-step German clothes care
2. Japanese comedian bombing
3. Description of a terrible joke
4. Grandfather clock
5. Late in getting joke
6. Nervous campers
7. Player aptitude during bonus split
8. When you need help to get to the orthopedic store
9. Overweight cello
10. Bad day with baseball and love
11. Guess as to how much you have in bank
12. Attraction for noise
13. Tripe in China
14. Anxious loom operator
15. Sailor's agreement

A. EAGER WEAVER
B. ORIENTRAILS
C. ONOMATAPPEAL
D. LAUGHTERTHOUGHT
E. IN TENTS
F. COMIKAZE
G. CRUTCH-22
H. GUFFAWFUL
I. INTERESTIMATE
J. SEE AYE TO AYE
K. WORLD SERIOUS
L. DREI CLEANING
M. NO RUNS, NO HITS, NO EROS
N. FAT AS A FIDDLE
O. OLD-TIMER

Answers: 1-L; 2-F; 3-H; 4-O; 5-D; 6-F; 7-K; 8-G; 9-N; 10-M; 11-I; 12-C; 13-B; 14-A; 15-J.

"Honey, come in here . . . I don't know, I think I'm too close to it."

MEWMEROLOGY

The PURRsonalysis of the Cats meow!

By Linus Maurer & Bill Dana —

CATISTICS TELL US THAT THERE ARE VERY FEW CASES OF CATSTROPHIC MENTAL ILLNESS REPORTED.

MEWMEROLOGY, THE PURRSONALITY ANALYSIS OF THE CAT'S MEOW, IS A MAJOR BREAKTHROUGH IN CATEGORIZING THE PUSSYCHOLOGICAL CONDITION OF YOUR OWN DEAR PET.

THE FOLLOWING PAGES WILL ENABLE YOU TO MAKE YOUR PURRSONAL PURRSONALYSIS.

WE ARE PUSSYMISTIC ABOUT YOUR SUCCESS SINCE OUR CATISTICS HAVE PROVEN TO BE 100% CORRECT 6% OF THE TIME.

WE HOPE THIS IS GOOD MEWS.

IF PUSSYCAT ONLY SAYS **ME**

THE MEOW DECADE HAS STRUCK AGAIN AND YOU HAVE A **MEGALOMANICAT**

THE SOUND **ME WHO? ME HOW?** IS SCATSOPHRENIC

A SURE SIGN OF THE **SPLIT PURR**SONALITY

TABBY OR NOT TABBY?... THAT IS THE QUESTION.

THE UTTERANCE **ME**

DENOTES **ANGORA**PHOBIA

FEAR OF SWEATERS

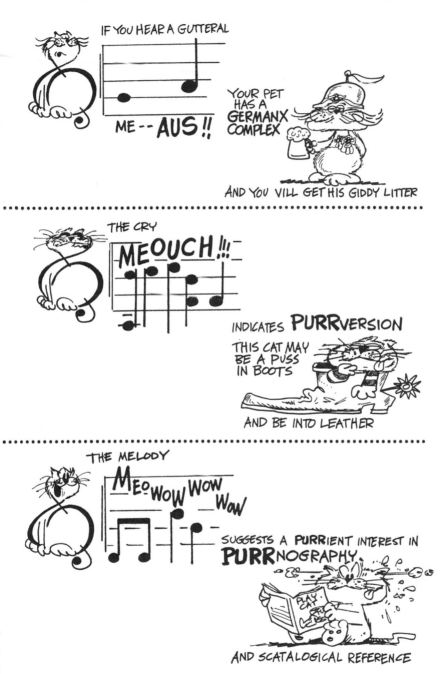

14.

Write Your Own Jokes

●●●

*My method is to take the
utmost trouble to find the
right thing to say, and then to
say it with the utmost levity.*
—GEORGE BERNARD SHAW

Not everyone can write humor—but not everyone can write a
novel, either. Most people think funny at times, and therefore are
capable of writing a gag, for a gag is just an expressed funny
thought. Writing humorous stories, essays, dialogue, cartoons,
poems, and so forth is complex and subtle work and is far
beyond the scope of this brief chapter. The discussion here will
be limited to how to put your senses of humor to work in
writing your own one-liners or jokes. Personalized or original
gags will enhance your letter writing, conversations, speeches
and problem solving. Two levels of gag writing will be described:
(1) personalizing jokes and (2) creating humor.

> *All I know about humor is that I don't know anything
> about it. Some bright boy over at NBC once told me
> there were only thirty-two basic jokes. Another bright
> boy reduced it to eleven. Somebody else has it down to
> two—comparison and exaggeration. Whatever it is, it
> never changes.*
> —FRED ALLEN

PERSONALIZING JOKES

If you are a comedian or an actor you might be capable of playing different characters or a variety of parts, and availing yourself of the opportunity to use and adapt a wide variety of comic material. In using humor in your conversation, in your letters, in social situations, on the job or to improve your speeches, you are not acting—you are you. Therefore, you should select jokes or gag lines that fit both your character and style of delivery.

The creation or adaptation of a gag can be best accomplished through actually writing it down. This gives you a better opportunity to change, to correct and to polish the line so that it will produce its best effect. This also makes it possible to keep a file of your best jokes. A joke file is a great asset if you wish to increase and improve your use of humor. Keeping your own file of personalized or original gags will help you become more aware of humor and more creative in its use. Most individuals who are spontaneously funny have a large store of humorous material that they recall and adapt quickly to suit the immediate situation. Spontaneity may consist of coming up with a completely new funny idea but usually consists of quick recall of an appropriate gag and the rapid adaptation of it so that it seems completely fresh.

I might say to my friends, "I worship the ground Irene walks on—and I'm also crazy about the property she owns in Palm Springs." I have done two things with this old gag. First, I have personalized it by using it as a first-person remark and by using my wife's name. Secondly, I have particularized it by identifying specifically where her real estate holdings are located. It does not matter for the sake of the joke whether she owns property or not. Whenever possible, be specific in naming people, objects and places. The effectiveness of a personalized, funny line is directly related to its relevance to the topic under discussion. This applies whether it is a conversation, lecture or committee meeting. A one-liner that doesn't seem very funny on the written page will get a favorable reception when it fits the situation. If your friends are lamenting the poor quality of today's service, you can say, "I was at Joe's Market yesterday and the clerk was so rude, I said to him, 'I'd like to remind you, sir, you are the overhead here, and I am the profit!' " Not only would this be an intelligent contribution to the discussion, but the humor of the remark would receive maximum appreciation and response. On the same subject, you could say, "Just yesterday I pulled into Sam's Station and the service was sure rotten. The dope that pumped the gas didn't check the oil, didn't clean the windshield, let the gas overflow and then forgot to replace the gas cap. And to make matters worse, the station is self-service!"

Occasionally, I am asked about how to write humor. I know that there is no way that I can give a satisfactory or helpful answer, so I paraphrase an old gag. "It's quite simple. There are only three rules for writing humor. The only problem is that nobody knows what they are." The brevity of these kinds of remarks almost assures their success. Most people will be amused to some degree so that even when the line does not get a big laugh, it does not cause the resentment a longer joke or story that fails to be hilarious would. So, in personalizing a gag or line that you have heard or read, work on it to eliminate any unnecessary words.

There is a place for the storyteller and for the longer joke or funny story, but personalizing gags and using them in an effective way requires more skill and work than does the one-liner. When you have one that meets the above criteria and that can be personalized by being directed at yourself, you have the winning combination.

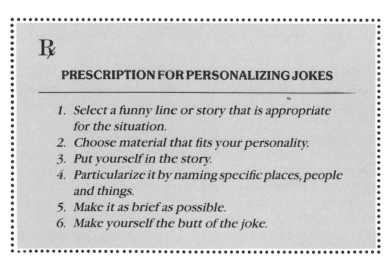

℞

PRESCRIPTION FOR PERSONALIZING JOKES

1. *Select a funny line or story that is appropriate for the situation.*
2. *Choose material that fits your personality.*
3. *Put yourself in the story.*
4. *Particularize it by naming specific places, people and things.*
5. *Make it as brief as possible.*
6. *Make yourself the butt of the joke.*

CREATING HUMOR

Incongruity is central to all humor. Something that does not fit the generally accepted mold—something out of context, unexpected, illogical, exaggerated, unreasonable or inappropriate—seems to be the essential element of humor.

> HUSBAND: This sexual permissiveness is disgusting. I just heard that the superintendent has had sex with every woman in this building except one.
>
> WIFE: And that one must be that stuck-up Mrs. Morris on the second floor.

The conventional expectation is for the wife to agree or disagree with her husband's disgust, and to claim that she is the innocent one. Instead, she attacks the one assumed to be innocent. The incongruity of the wife's response, when she is provided with the opportunity to claim that she is the innocent one, provides the essential humor of the joke.

Other humorous elements also contribute to the effectiveness of a joke, story, poem, essay or cartoon. The writing and presentations, as well as the appropriateness of the material, all contribute to the humorous effect. Incongruity is not humor in and of itself. A tragic, unexpected accident is not funny. Although incongruity is the foundation of humor, it is not the whole structure.

> *Humor is emotional chaos remembered in tranquility.*
> **—JAMES THURBER**

To see the humor in tragedy, or the tragedy in what is conventionally accepted as pleasant, requires an attitude of playfulness, or what is referred to as the *comic sense*. This attitude may bring forth a funny thought at almost any time or in any place. You could be shopping, working, driving, reading or listening to a presidential address when the comic spirit strikes. When this happens, that part of you called your sense of humor takes off and takes a different view of what you are watching, listening to, reading or thinking about. This different view is the basis of your conceiving a funny idea. It is impossible for me to tell you how to come up with a funny idea, but I can provide you with

activities that will assist in developing your ability to conceive
and write original funny stuff.

I don't know what humor is. Anything that's funny—
tragedy or anything, it don't make no difference so
[long as] you happen to hit it just right. But there's one
thing I'm proud of—I ain't got it in for anybody. I don't
like to make jokes that hurt anybody.

—WILL ROGERS

The comic sense, when set free, may enable you to come up
with funny stuff that is hostile, ribald, sick, wise, witty or nonsensical. It is up to you to decide what to do with it after you've
got it. If you, like Will Rogers, don't want to deal in hostile or
aggressive humor, you will reject the funny idea rather than
develop it into sick humor or an insulting joke. You will look
instead for a gentler idea. If you come up with a ribald idea about
sexual activity, but don't want to produce sexual humor, you will
not develop the idea into a sex gag. If you wish to develop your
sense of humor and the ability to originate the humorous material,
you must give your comic sense free reign. You can decide what
you want to do with the funny stuff your sense of humor produces, but you must not try to control or censure what it does.

Once you have a funny idea, how do you write a gag? What do
you do with an idea after you've got it? First, articulate it—spell
it out, write it down or, at least, talk to yourself about it and
listen critically. Make sure it is a funny concept that can be
communicated. Second, condense it into as few words as possible. Work with your idea, stretch it to the point of ridiculousness,
twist it, juggle the words around, chop and change until you
have the tightest, funniest arrangement possible.

The simplest way to start writing funny lines is to rework
familiar material—like old sayings, proverbs or epigrams. Let's
start with the old proverb, "A bird in the hand is worth two in
the bush," and rewrite the ending. "A bird in the hand is finger
licking good." The familiar proverb establishes an expectation of
the conventional ending and the new ending abruptly changes
direction from that expectation so that we are confronted with
incongruity. By starting your writing of jokes with familiar lines
or ideas and letting your comic sense provide funny changes,
you do not need to establish a story line or set the direction. You

only have to produce the change in direction or the incongruity. "A bird in the hand is—messy." "Two in the bush is the root of all evil."

Where there's life there's hope—for one more medical bill.

Give a man enough rope—and he'll fill the house with potted plants in weird looking macrame hangers.

When the going gets tough, the tough—steal.

The paths of glory lead but to the grave—so do all other paths.

Live each day as if it were your last—someday you'll be right.

A stitch in time saves—embarrassment.

The meek shall inherit the earth—but not the oil rights.

Do unto others—then run.

A friend in need is a—damn nuisance.

A man's home is his hassle.

'Tis better to have loved and lost than to end up doing dishes twenty times a week.

Cleanliness is next to—impossible.

After you have rewritten some well-known sayings, try reworking some conventional ideas.

Television was better in the old days—before it had pictures and sound.

Pick a winner. Anyone can pick a loser.

The light at the end of the tunnel could be the headlight of an oncoming train.

If you can fool all of the people some of the time—that's enough to get elected.

Let your accountant not your conscience be your guide.

I think modern art proves that things are not as bad as they are painted.

Some of our great wits and writers have produced their best

lines through simply changing the wording of old sayings or playing with conventional ideas.

> *The race is not always to the swift, nor the battle to the strong —but that's the way to bet.*
> — DAMON RUNYON

> *The ship of state is the only known vessel that leaks from the top.*
> — JAMES RESTON

> *To err is human, but it feels divine.*
> — MAE WEST

> *My heart is as pure as the driven slush.*
> — TALLULAH BANKHEAD

> *I am free of all prejudices. I hate everybody equally.*
> — W. C. FIELDS

Satire is humor with a serious purpose. Most humor is intended to make you laugh and relax, while satire is intended to make you laugh and think. The pendulum of satire may swing from the bitter genius of Mark Twain and Ambrose Bierce to the more gentle, and often as effective, offerings of Art Buchwald and Erma Bombeck.

As a teenager I collected quotations, most of which were of the witty, one-line type. My favorites were the brief, daily columns written by Frank McKinney ("Kin") Hubbard. He was able to express all he wanted to say on a subject in so few words that he produced the shortest newspaper column on record. Each consisted of one sentence.

> Miss Linnet Spry was confined to her home with a swollen dresser drawer.

> Miss Germ Williams is just a natural-born artist and draws her portraits on ruled paper so she can keep the ears even.

> I'll bet the hardest thing about prize fighting is picking up your teeth with boxing gloves on.

What impressed me most was his tricking the reader into providing the answer to what Miss Spry kept in her dresser drawer, what Miss Williams' portraits were really like, or the other hazards of boxing.

Many years later, when I wrote The Peter Principle: In a hierarchy individuals tend to rise to their levels of incompetence, I received thousands of letters. Most of them contained case studies of the principle in action—stories about individuals who had reached their levels of incompetence: competent students who became incompetent teachers, competent salesmen who became incompetent sales managers and competent followers who became incompetent leaders. I then realized that although my laws and principles appeared to have little similarity to Kin Hubbard's columns, they, too, involved the reader in doing the detail work.

> Peter's Laugh-In Principle: When the boss tells a joke, he who laughs lasts.

> Peter's Educational Law: Experience is the worst teacher—it gives the test before explaining the lesson.

> Peter's Differential Diagnosis: There are two kinds of losers: the good loser and those who can't act.

> Peter's Marriage Law: All marriages are happy, but living together afterward can be troublesome.

> Peter's Child Development Principle: Children grow up quickly these days—many teenagers are already confused, discouraged and broke.

> Peter's Laughter Principle: A sense of humor is what makes you laugh at things that would annoy you if they happened to you.

> Peter's Bureaucratic Principle: Bureaucracy defends the status quo long past the time when the quo has lost its status.

> Peter's Principle of Peak Experience: Climb the ladder of success, reach the top and you'll find you're over the hill.

> The Peter Sexist Principle: Most hierarchies were established by men who now monopolize the upper levels, thus depriving women of their rightful share of opportunities for achieving their own levels of incompetence.

So far, we have been examining how to write humor that in

one way or another tries to get at the truth. Nonsense, humor and word play that exist purely for entertainment value can be created in the same way as humor that may have a more serious purpose. "A stitch in time is worth two in the bush," may seem funny because of its lack of meaning.

"Did we meet in Chicago?"

"I've never been in Chicago."

"Neither have I. It probably was two other guys."

There is incongruity and lack of logic in this conversation, although the structure is the same as that of a logical question-and-answer dialogue. Similarly, a nonsense poem looks and sounds like a meaningful verse.

SNAVELY'S POEM

How pierceful grows the hazy yon
How mertle petails thou,
For spring has sprung the cyclotron
How high browse thou Brown cow?
—WALT KELLY

There are many types of word play you can engage in for laughs or groans, the pun being the most popular. Punning is exchanging words that sound familiar but have different meanings.

Hanging is too good for a man who makes puns; he should be drawn and quoted.

—Fred Allen

Schubert had a horse named Sarah.
He drove her to the big parade
And all the time the band was playing,
Schubert's Sarah neighed.

When I am dead, I hope it may be said,
"His sins were scarlet, but his books were read."

—Hilaire Belloc

"Dr. Jekyll, tell me about your alter ego."
"No, you're getting under my Hyde."

At the New York Public Library you can "Read between the lions."

"Dear Abby, I would like to know how long girls should be courted."
"The same as short girls."

The cop hit the demonstrator on the head. A bystander remarked, "He conks to stupor."

A type of word play that I enjoy points at the incongruity of our conventional use of words. We say "stop-and-go traffic," but we should say go-and-stop because we have to go before we can stop. "Change our plans" and "alter our plans" mean the same thing, but "change our pants" and "alter our pants" mean quite different things. We say "boned chicken" when we mean deboned chicken and we say "flammable" and "inflammable" when we mean the same thing. This may all sound farfetched to you, but that's because nothing is ever near-fetched.

> *In two words: im possible.*
>
> —SAMUEL GOLDWYN

Today paper prices are rising and time is of the essence but we still waste paper space and time with redundancies. We read about "free gifts," "extra bonuses" and "desirable benefits." Our politicians begin their speeches with such repetition as "Let me preface my opening remarks with a preamble," and then they go on to tell "each and every one" that they "over and above" everything else promise that by "advance planning" to be able to "plan ahead" and avoid "vacillating back and forth," so as to achieve "lasting, long-term results." As the typical political speech proceeds, it includes references to "puzzling riddles," "unsolved problems," "the big, major issues," "the present incumbent," "other alternatives," "qualified experts," "complete monopolies," "preparations ahead of time," "true facts," "opponents against the plan" and an appeal for "one and all" to "join together for one single purpose" to eliminate redundancy in government.

If you had paid attention when Gerald Ford said, "Sole and single purpose" or when Goodwin Knight said, "The future lies ahead," or when Jimmy Carter said, "Convincingly persuasive," today you might be either a comedy writer or a political speech writer.

> *There's no trick to being a humorist when you have the whole government working for you.*
>
> —WILL ROGERS.

In this brief discussion of how to create and write jokes, we have looked at some ways to get started. I have used these methods with students, and many who had never written a gag line were able to start right in by producing funny endings for old sayings and familiar television commercials. If you wish to have further guidance in your humor writing, there are books available. One of my favorites is *Intent on Laughter* by John Bailey, because it is a funny book about being funny which includes descriptions of just about every form of humor, exaggeration, word play, humorous verse, satire, caricature and cartoons.

BECOMING UNKNOWN

THE UNKNOWN COMIC'S METHOD
OF BECOMING UNKNOWN*

To attain a state of complete anonymity, simply repeat these one-liners, one section at a time.

SECTION I

Hear about the 500-pound parrot? It says, "Polly wants a cracker, NOW!!"

Last week Bo Derek asked me out. I was in her house at the time.

A bum came up to me outside the Waldorf...that's where I live, outside the Waldorf. The bum said, "I haven't eaten in three days." I said, "That's terrible. Force yourself."

A friend of mine crossed a polar bear with a python. He doesn't know what he's got but it makes a great rug for a long thin hallway.

Another guy crossed a parakeet with a hippopotamus: the darned thing broke its wings trying to take off.

There's gonna be a new TV show sponsored by Hebrew National Salami. It's called "Press the Meat."

Wanna drive your husband crazy? Smile in your sleep.

I crossed an octopus with a bale of hay. Got a broom with eight handles.

If you are still known, repeat Section II:

SECTION II

I don't want to say my brother-in-law is dumb, but he's got "T.G.I.F." on his slippers: "Toes Go In First."

I just paid my taxes and my wallet has been declared legally dead.

You know why a hummingbird hums? Because he don't know the words.

I don't want to say my brother-in-law has a booze problem, but once a year he lays a wreath on the tomb of the Unknown Drunk.

If Astroturf was poison ivy—what a case of jock itch!

I entertained my wife last night. Unfortunately, it was by being beat up.

It's true that money talks; mine just said good-bye.

*Murray Langston's Unknown Comic Scrapbag, Bill Dana, Bantam Books, New York, 1981.

When all else fails, try these:

SECTION III

My wife had an accident; she now owns a Mercedes-Bent.

I have a cousin who looks just like Dolly Parton. He's the most popular cadet at West Point.

I have a friend who is so rich that when he grew up his parents had his nanny bronzed.

You know it wasn't until I was thirty-five that I realized that girls were a dime a dozen—up until then I was buying jelly beans.

Let a smile be your umbrella...it keeps your chin dry in a hurricane.

My new car has bucket seats —they're really comfortable as long as your bucket ain't too big.

My chick made a dress out of odds and ends. It sure is odd where it ends.

Do you know that sdrawkcab is "backwards" spelled backwards?

I'll never forget when my pop caught me smoking...boy, did he yell at the kid who set me on fire!

My grandfather appreciates booze...you don't have to chew it.

IF YOU ARE STILL KNOWN AFTER ALL THREE SECTIONS, PLACE HEAD IN PAPER BAG AND WAIT FOR INSTRUCTIONS.

No matter what you call it

A FORMULA IS
A FORMULA IS
A FORMULA

●●

Back in the early '50s, Leonard Stern, the late Don Hinkley and I concocted a way of doing jokes by delivering the punchline first and giving the set-up. We called it THE QUESTION MAN. We developed the excuse that today, everybody knows all the answers. As a matter of fact, there are more answers than there are questions. So, to fill in the gap, Steve Allen as The Question Man would provide questions for these superfluous answers. Somewhere along the line Johnny Carson commenced using the same premise to extremely funny advantage. Johnny's formula was called KARNAK. The game show "Jeopardy" used the same formula in its intelligent way. So, we see that with comedy formulae, it ain't whacha do, it's the way acha do it.

Just for the fun of it and also to get you into a learn-while-game-playing mode, try the following matchups. Let's call our game QUESTNAKORDY.

—B.D.

A. CHICKEN TERIYAKI
B. 9-W
C. THE NINA, THE PINTA AND
   THE SANTA MARIA
D. HART, SHAFFNER AND MARX
E. NO, EGG FOO YUNG
F. IGLOO
G. LOOK FOR THE UNION LABEL
H. JIGSAW PUZZLES,
   MARRIAGES AND
   AMERICAN-MADE CARS
I. OIL
J. TRICKLE DOWN
K. FORTUNE HUNTER
L. THE WRONG STUFF
M. EGGS McMUFFIN
N. PILOT LIGHT
O. VINCENT VAN STAY
P. MURPHY'S SENTENCE
Q. KU KLUX KOHEN
R. GENE TRANSPLANT
S. PRIVATE EYE
T. PROFITS
U. THE GOOD PARTS

1. Name three Italian restaurants.
2. What did Murphy get for breaking his law?
3. Name three Italian restaurant owners.
4. What do you use to stick Igs together?
5. Give the name of the book about flunked-out astronauts.
6. Name a cult that didn't make it.
7. Do you spell Wagner with a V?
8. Name Tab's rich uncle.
9. Name three things that always fall apart.
10. What is the first clue for finding Jimmy Hoffa?
11. What do you stuff a trickle with?
12. What do you call what causes smog?
13. What is Bo Derek's sister's name?
14. What do you call exchanging a Wilder for a Rayburn?
15. What is Grandma identifying when she dog-ears her Bible?
16. Is Egg Foo old?
17. Who is the oldest kamikaze pilot?
18. Name an Irish crook.
19. What would you call your peepee if you could see through it?
20. Name an artist with two ears.
21. What's a good thing to burn test scripts?

ANSWERS: A-17; B-7; C-1; D-3; E-16; F-4; G-10; H-9; I-13; J-11; K-8;
L-5; M-18; N-21; O-20; P-2; Q-6; R-14; S-19; T-12; U-15.

MATCHING TWO-LINERS

MATCH THE JOKE WITH ITS PUNCHLINE.*

●●●

A. How can men live without women?

B. Do you know the wages of sin are death?

C. Do you remember the name of that circus guy who used to stick his right arm in the lion's mouth?

D. Why do you like nudist weddings?

E. So that's not a complex?

F. I have only ten minutes and I don't know where to begin.

G. That college student can run and block.

H. When is your sister Harriet thinking of getting married?

I. Did the noise bother you last night when my boyfriend was here?

J. Your son is a bigger tipper than you.

K. Do you know how to make air travel safer?

L. Why are people in big cities so rude?

M. I hear you dated Siamese twins. Did you have a good time?

N. I hear you bought a two-story house.

1. Lefty.
2. Because I always know who the best man is.
3. Cheaper.
4. No, you actually are inferior.
5. No, hum the first few bars.
6. Shame he couldn't pass.
7. Constantly.
8. No, the silence did.
9. Begin at the ninth.
10. He has a wealthy father, I don't.
11. They don't want to be mistaken for visitors.
12. Yeah, the broker told me one story before I bought it and a different one afterward.
13. Yes and no.
14. Sure, eliminate the car ride from the home to the airport.

*ANSWERS: A-3; B-5; C-1; D-2; E-4; F-9; G-6; H-7; I-8; J-10; K-14; L-11; M-13; N-12.

PUNGEONS AND DRAGONS

Certain jokes are generic. A clever joke writer and/or joke user can twist various joke formulas and make them fit any requirements. Here's an example of taking classic and semiclassic standards and fitting them into a new and trendy mode. They are excerpts from:

PUNGEONS
AND
DRAGONS

•••

See if you can identify the jokes that have been twisted for Arthur's sake.

"Doth this shield belong to you? The name is obliterated."
"It cannot then be mine. My name is Llewelyn."

•

A knight-at-arms was instructing pages aspiring to knighthood in the use of the lance.
   "This device will penetrate solid wood. So keep your heads down."

•

Two steeds from Camelot were discussing the next day's joust:
   "This is a very important joust. The winner's horse will get many bales of hay, and that ain't money."

•

Two knights walked into an imbibing room. They looked in vain for the attendant. Finally a horse emerged from behind the counter.
   "What do you wish, sires?"
The two knights were aghast and stared at this seeming witchery speechless. The horse spake:

"What are you staring at?"
"The dragon sold the place???"

•

An underachiever page was applying for a knight attendant's position. On the employment scroll, after the question "Age" he wrote: "Dark."

•

If you think old knights fade away, try getting into your old armour.

•

Two maidens were admiring some mounted knights who were passing. A particularly proud and haughty knight passed by.
   "Yon knight stirreth something within me. Observe how handsome he is in his shining armour."
An older and more sage companion added:
   "He seemeth promising from the outside. But I know a squire who owns a ten-steed stable and has nothing in it but a plough."

Sir Ernest met his demise whilst fighting Modred's men. In his tomb, a male and female worm met. The male worm spaketh:

"Let's make love in dead Ernest."

•

"Be careful with your aim, archer, you almost hit my wife."
"My deepest apologies, sire, take a shot at yon wench. She's *my* wife."

•

Sign on Camelot bulletin board:
Handmaiden desires job. No bad habits. Willing to learn.

A drunken knight to his fellow carouser:

"Won't your wife hit the ceiling when you get home?"
"I hope so. Last time she put an arrow through my helmet."

•

"Are you the widow of Sir Morris?"
"I am the wife of Sir Morris, not his widow."
"Oh, no? Take a look at what's strapped to yon horse."

15.

Perform for Laughs

●●

Life is a joke that's just begun.
—W.S. GILBERT

Get a laugh and you've made a friend. Whether you are speaking in public or in simple conversation, the ability to provoke laughter is one of your greatest assets.

SUGGESTED GUIDELINES

Don't tell any joke unless you are sold on it yourself. Don't take chances by doubting your material. Rely on your first impression of the joke's humor. Question the appropriateness of the humor. Consider the propriety of racial, sexual and ethnic stereotypes.

There is no joke that will not offend someone, no matter how innocent your intent. Hence it is your job to evaluate your audience and the potential for possible offensiveness.

Tragedy plus time equals comedy.
—STEVE ALLEN

The day after Lincoln's assassination, you would have suffered a fate similar to the former president's if you had said, "Other than that, Mrs. Lincoln, how did you like the play?"

A man will confess to treason, murder, arson, false teeth, or a wig. How many of them will own up to a lack of humor.
—FRANK MOORE COLBY

221 ·

When you tell a story, give the impression that you are enjoying yourself. In telling your joke, keep your tone conversational and your choice of words and sentence construction completely natural. Speak in a down-to-earth style with which your listeners will feel comfortable.

TELLING JOKES

In telling a joke, there is nothing more important than your listeners hearing exactly what you are saying. If they miss one key word, chances are your joke will fall flat and you can do little to rescue it. Attempts at repeating jokes are seldom successful. You can take a cue from professional comedians and develop a recovery technique. Johnny Carson, who is today's foremost exponent of recovery humor, usually blames the audience when a joke flops by suggesting either that the audience is turning against him or that they are asleep, drunk, stoned or all of the above. This type of recovery, although it appears simple, requires highly developed comic skill. Usually, it is best to ignore the bomb or blame yourself for the explosion.

> *I had my nose fixed, now my mouth won't work.*
>
> —MILTON BERLE

When Uncle Miltie makes his famous recovery line, he underscores another vital aspect of successful joke-telling: *any* interruption can steal your thunder. If you listen to a professional speaker or comedian, you will notice that he/she will protect himself/herself from even the slightest interruption—a sneeze, a baby's cry or a slammed door—by repeating those words that may have been missed. It is interesting to observe just how fragile a joke is. Anyone who has experienced a waiter appearing on the punchline knows that if you don't back up and start over, your joke is doomed.

It's a good idea to have a portable tape recorder handy every time you give a speech, so that you can have a record of your thrills of victory and your agonies of defeat. Using a tape recorder will help you analyze your style. You should ask yourself the basic question, "What will the audience accept from me?" Imagine a person with an inappropriate style trying to do Don

Rickles-type put-down humor. You will learn from experience what you can "get away with" or what you can't. Your style gives you the license for the type of material you can handle. It is important that you understand your audience's perception of you, whether you are telling a joke to a group of friends or addressing a large audience. That is the vital determinant of your material. We've all heard someone remark, "When you say that, it sounds so cute. If I said that, I'd get my face slapped!"

A tape recording will also help you analyze your timing. The observation that timing is the essence of comedy should be amended to: *your own* timing is the essence of your comedy. Experimenting will provide you with the answers. There are many avenues of pacing and timing you can use to arrive at a punchline. It's up to you to determine your best route. I have found that reviewing tapes of my lectures helps me settle into a specific timing. Here are a few examples of what works for me:

"Mr. Chairman, thank you for that *warm reception.* In all sincerity, I want to say that of all the introductions I have ever had, that was the most (pause) *recent.*"

"I especially admire your way with words and the way you don't let yourself be inhibited by (pause) *the facts.*"

"I'm very *happy* to be here tonight. In fact, at *my age* I'm happy to be (pause) *anywhere.*"

"Being sixty–five isn't so bad. The way things have been going for me, being called a (slight pause) *sexagenarian* (slight pause) sounds like (pause) *flattery.*"

"Science has made great strides—now it's only twenty years *behind* (pause) the *comic books.*"

"The *inflation* has transformed my (slight pause) *nest egg* (slight pause) into a (pause) *goose egg.*"

"I spent my *vacation* in my own *back yard.* It showed my neighbors the *kind of person I am*—practical, imaginative, home-loving and (pause) *broke.*"

"I like to go to the *drive-in bank.* (pause) Let's my car see its (pause) *real owner.*"

Practice and your joke-telling skill will improve, but beyond this the most important learning device is feedback. Do your homework. Through practice you will become proficient. It is through feedback—your listeners' responses—that you will learn the complex and subtle aspects of making people laugh. It is your sensitivity to effectiveness in provoking laughter that will teach you those things that can only be learned by experience. Watch your listeners. Let your observations tell you what works best. Try being deadpan when you deliver your punchline. Try smiling. Look surprised when they laugh. Try different gestures. Your listeners will tell you what is right for you. This sensitivity to your audience's responses is your best teacher.

℞

PETER'S PRESCRIPTION FOR JOKE TELLERS

1. *Use jokes that you believe in—gags that really amused you the first time you heard them or the first time you thought of them.*
   Caution: Be careful in selecting jokes that will be appropriate for the time, place and audience.
2. *Use a conversational tone in delivering your jokes. Speak clearly and project without shouting. Avoid dialect stories, unless you are really proficient in dialects.*
3. *If a joke fails to get a laugh, either continue with your talk or turn the joke on yourself by using a gag about why you failed.*
4. *Emphasize the key words and phrases in your buildup and deliver the punchline with deliberation.*
5. *Study your timing so that your joke is paced precisely and the punchline is delivered after a pause just long enough to heighten the listener's expectations.*
6. *Be sensitive to your listeners' responses, so that every time you tell a joke it is a learning experience for you.*

ARE YOU QUALIFIED TO BE A STAND-UP COMEDIAN?

TAKE THIS SIMPLE TEST.

Good evening, ladies and gentlemen. I call you ladies and gentlemen
- A. because you seem quite nice.
- B. you know what you are.
- C. since there are too many of you to identify individually by name.

I just flew in from Chicago,
- A. and, boy, are my arms tired.
- B. and it was quite pleasant on the plane.
- C. and I'm going back soon.

The last time I played here, they had the ropes up.
- A. That's how good business was.
- B. But, there was no need for that tonight.
- C. The boss was hanging himself.

I thought business was bad but at nine o'clock a party of seventy came in.
- A. Nice old man. He sat right there.
- B. I guess they were celebrating something.
- C. Quite a big group for here.

I'll tell you how business is here. It's usually slow until midnight.
- A. Then a lot of times the late crowd shows up.
- B. Which is disappointing.
- C. Then, it falls off.

Hey, I don't have to do this for a living.
- A. I have an Amway distributorship.
- B. My wife is fairly well-to-do.
- C. I could starve.

Take my wife
- A. for example.
- B. with you if you're going someplace interesting.
- C. please.

That place was so dirty
- A. it should have been condemned.
- B. it was darned unpleasant.
- C. even the mice had athlete's foot.

She was so fat
- A. it must've been unhealthy.
- B. she should have gone on a strict diet.
- C. when she sat down she had to make two trips.

225 ·

He's so old
  A. he has a lot of wrinkles.
  B. but still quite sharp.
  C. he uses Absorbine Senior.

Well, goodnight, and don't forget,
if you're driving home
  A. be very careful.
  B. don't drink excessively.
  C. take a car.

I know you're out there.
  A. The stage manager informed
     me of your presence.
  B. I can see quite well despite
     the spotlight.
  C. I can hear you breathing.

What is that out there?
  A. A painting?
  B. A lot of bored people?
  C. An inattentive audience?

SIMPLE SCORING PROCEDURE. If you had any trouble deciding on any answer, you are not qualified to be a stand-up comedian, but you do qualify for handicapped parking at The Comedy Store.

16.

Peter's Pharmacy

●●

Create Your Own
Humorous Life Style

1. Discover the power of humor.
2. Write your own humorous material.
3. Tell jokes for big laughs.

BOOKS

Laughter and Liberation: Developing Your Sense of Humor, the Psychology of Laughter, Harvey Mindess. Nash Publishing, 1971. Available from: Harvey Mindess, Ph.D., 337 South Beverly Drive, Beverly Hills, California 90212.

Harvey Mindess tells how laughter and our sense of humor work and how they may be cultivated. "Once we have acquired the ability to take things seriously, we need to revive the ability to take them playfully." Mindess shows how laughter can liberate us from fear, sorrow, tension and inhibition—or extricate us from awkward, terrifying or uncomfortable situations. Rich with humorous examples, this book bears not just reading, but re-reading.

Humor: Its Origin and Development, Paul E. McGhee. Texas Technical University, W.H. Freeman and Company, San Francisco, California, 1979.

The author brings together current research on how children develop a sense of humor. He explores how a child learns to appreciate and create humor as he/she develops certain cognitive skills. Dr. McGhee also discusses humor as a clinical tool and as a way for children to cope with problems. Although the book is a psychological treatment of the subject, no specialized background is required of the reader.

The Enjoyment of Laughter, Max Eastman. Simon and Schuster, New York, 1938.

This is the classic work on humor. The author explains why we laugh, describes the various theories of humor and classifies types of humor, and explores each through presentation of hundreds of examples. Descriptions of humor by practicing humorists are included. Although many of the examples are outdated, this book remains the best and most comprehensive treatment of the subject.

Intent on Laughter, John Bailey. Quadrangle/Times Books, New York, 1976.

The author, former humor editor for the *Saturday Evening Post*, reveals some of the tricks of the humor trade. Although no book can impart the comic sense that is the wellspring of funny ideas, this one does a good job of showing what the comic or humorist goes through in developing the finished product. The author claims that the humorist, just as a chemist, is subject to a set of rules that can be learned. To prove the point he suggests a little experiment that readers can try.
1. Pour a little hydrochloric acid in a saucer.
2. Stir it with your finger.
3. Notice how much shorter your finger is.
The book contains illustrative examples of each type of humor discussed and includes instructions for and examples of cartooning.

The Comic Encyclopedia, Evan Esar. Doubleday & Company, Inc., Garden City, New York, 1978.

This is truly an encyclopedia. It contains 829 pages of alphabetical-ly listed information including the history, literature and definitions of humor, along with thousands of gags, sayings and anecdotes whose range is enormous. Included are explanations of the science and practice of comedy. As a reference work or as a text for the student of humor, this book is one of a kind.

Peter's People, and Their Marvelous Ideas, Laurence J. Peter. William Morrow and Company, Inc., New York, 1979.

This is a book of satirical essays about people from the past and present whose lives and accomplishments are important to our time. In addition to the humorous profiles of such celebrities as Johnny Carson, Thomas Crapper and Richard Nixon, the book contains imaginary interviews with such persons from our past as Benjamin Franklin, Mark Twain and Will Rogers. All of their answers to the author's questions were selected from their actual words, whether written or spoken. The book also contains 498 laws that help one explain, or at least laugh at, the human condition.

AUDIO TAPES

Listening analytically to taped performances of master comedians can be a practical means of improving your own joke-telling ability. In the case of those who use humor relevant to real-life situations, listening can assist in your development of a humorous outlook. Of the many comedians' work currently available on cassette, here are a few that you may feel are worth your time and may brighten your trip to work some mornings:

Franklyn Ajaye, *Don't Smoke Dope* (Little David CS–1011); Archie Campbell, *Good Humor Man* (Elektra TC 5–1075); George Carlin, *Class Clown* (Little David CS–1004), *Evening with Wally* (Little David CS–1008), *Indecent Exposure* (Little David CS–1076), *Occupation Foole* (Little David CS–1005), *On the Road* (Little David CS–1075); Cheech and Chong, *Big Bambu* (Warner M–53251), *Los Cochinos* (Warner M–53252), *Let's Make a New Deal* (Warner W5–3391), *Wedding Album* (Warner M–5353); Jerry Clower, *Ain't God Good* (Word WC–8737), *Grand Ole Opry!* (MCA G3062), *Mississippi Talkin'* (MCA C–33); Bill Cosby, *Bill's Best Friend* (Capital 4XT– 11731), *For Adults Only* (MCA, C–553); W.C. Fields, *Voicetracks* (MCA, C–2073); Gallagher, *Gallagher* (United Artists 4LT–1019); Bob Harrington, *Have Fun with Me* (Canaan CC–9744); Bob Hope, *America is 200 Years Old* (Capital 4XT– 11538); Steve Martin, *Comedy is Not Pretty* (Warner W53392); Groucho Marx, *An Evening with Groucho Marx* (A&M CS–3515); Martin Mull, *Near Perfect* (Electra TC 5– 200); Richard Pryor, *Bicentennial Nigger* (Warner M53114), *Is It Something* (Reprise M52285), *Nigger Crazy* (Reprise M52287); Hal Roach, *Irish Humor* (Rego 14000); Father Guido Sarducci, *Live at St. Douglas Convent* (Warner M53440); Robin Williams, *Reality — What a Concept* (Casablanca 5–7162).

ABOUT THE AUTHORS

Laurence J. Peter was born to poor but pompous parents in his native province of British Columbia, Canada, where he received an extensive but inadequate education.

His professional life has been devoted to teaching and to research into teacher competence. His studies of competence revealed many examples of incompetence. He used these examples as comic relief when presenting his competence research. Ultimately this lead to his writing a satirical trilogy on the subject of incompetence— *The Peter Principle, The Peter Prescription* and *The Peter Plan*.

Throughout his career in education he has studied the effects of humor in teaching, communications and problem solving. With the publication of *The Laughter Prescription*, Dr. Peter continues his campaign to save the human race from the perils of the Peter Principle.

William Szathmary was born to poor but poverty-stricken parents in Quincy, Massachusetts. Bill Dana was born in Showbiz, New York 10019. Early in his career, Bill and Don Adams created the character that eventually became Maxwell Smart. Then Bill went on to write for Steve Allen's legendary "Tonight Show." It was on Steve's show in 1959 where José Jimenez was born. The rest is history. *We, Seven* by the original astronauts, *The Right Stuff*, book and movie, the Smithsonian Institution, and James Michener's *Space* all credit José's Light Stuff as an important Laughter Prescription for America's first space adventure.

It is Bill's background of three decades writing some of the most creative comedy in the history of television upon which he draws the "written, remembered and arranged" humor segments of *The Laughter Prescription*.